THE BEST PUBS IN LONDON

A tavern ...is the busy man's recreation, the idle man's business, the melancholy man's sanctuary, the stranger's welcome, the Inns of Court man's entertainment, the scholar's kindness and the citizen's courtesy.

— John Earle, 1628.

D0308486

ALSO BY ROGER PROTZ

Pulling a Fast One (What the Brewers Have
Done to Your Beer)

Capital Ale

The Good Beer Guide (*editor*) 1978–1983

Beer, Bed and Breakfast (*editor*) 1986/1988

The Great British Beer Book

The author wishes to thank all those members
of CAMRA who recommended pubs for this
guide. He is responsible for the final selection.
He also thanks Martyn Cornell of the Brewery
History Society for advice – and a pint – about
the history of brewing in London.

THE BEST PUBS IN
London

Roger Protz

Illustrated by Phil Evans

ALMA
BOOKS

IN ASSOCIATION WITH THE
CAMPAIGN FOR REAL ALE

Author: **Roger Protz**

Design: **Opus**

Illustrations: **Phil Evans**

Cover photograph of the Founder's Arms: **Chris Honeywell**

Typeset and printed by: **Cambridge University Press**

ISBN 1–85249–014–4

Published by **Alma Books Ltd.**, a wholly-owned subsidiary of the Campaign for Real Ale Ltd., 34 Alma Road, St Albans, Herts.

CONTENTS

The Argyll Arms, Argyll Street, Oxford Circus

INTRODUCTION

This book is not so much a guide, more a celebration of the London pub. To call the pub an institution is not to indulge in hyperbole. Its roots are deep in British society. It has evolved slowly and ruminatively over many centuries, from the Saxon alehouse, the medieval tavern and inn, to the Victorian concept of the "public house" which we have reduced to a shorthand form that is recognised throughout the world. High on the list of every visitor to London, vying with spotting a red bus or being fleeced in a black taxi, is a trip to a pub. They stand on almost every corner, not anonymously like a Continental café or skulking underground like a *bierkeller*, but proudly displaying their inn signs and an architectural style that ranges from genuine Elizabethan to mock "brewer's Tudor".

The "best" London pubs are not just those confined to the centre of the capital. There are many famous pubs in this guide but there are also many lesser known ones, some tucked away in side streets and suburbs. To be good is not the same as being well-known and there are pubs in these pages that will never grace other guide books but which deserve their place here because they embody everything that a good pub should be: the welcome is genuine, the natives are friendly, the ale is good and the food, however rudimentary, is ample, fresh and home-cooked.

Do not expect to find history in every pub. There are few old Elizabethan inns like the George at Southwark still surviving. Most inns of that period were destroyed in the Great Fire of London in 1666 and their successors over the centuries have fallen down through age or neglect, or have made way for houses, factories and offices. Most London pubs do not go back any further than the late 19th century and, as Horniman's at Hays Wharf and the Founder's Arms on Bankside show, many exciting concepts are being developed in the latter part of the twentieth century.

Ten per cent of Britain's seventy thousand pubs reside within the boundaries of the county of Greater London. Just a tiny fraction of that number has been chosen for this guide. It is a selection, and a subjective one at that, of what I consider to be the best, with as much information about each one as time and space allow.

PUBS UNDER ATTACK

The guide could be sub-titled "In Defence of the London Pub" for what is celebrated here is under sustained and calculated attack. The desecration of the London pub is part of the London-wide challenge to the capital's fine buildings and architecture. Stand on any one of the great London bridges, look to right or left, and see what havoc is being done to a once noble shoreline and skyline by ugly modern concrete constructions that have all the charm and elegance of the average Paris *pissoir*.

The same vandals and architectural Visigoths are at work on the London pub. Scores of pleasant and inoffensive pubs have been torn apart as some mad marketing nightmare is visited on them. Builders, plumbers and decorators descend and after a week or two of whirlwind activity new "theme" pubs or – to use the marketing jargon – "café-bars" appear in their place. Instead of the Fox or the Shakespeare or the George IV we get Drummonds, Le Dôme or Presleys. *In extremis* we are even faced with the last word in insensitive bad taste, a bar called Blitz designed like a nuclear fall-out shelter.

Such madness is not demanded by customers.

Large breweries, with more money than sense, employ people to conduct "demographic sweeps" of entire areas. They talk not of customers but of "traffic"; pubs become "profit centres". If, in their ineffable wisdom, the majority of "traffic" in any given area is composed of youngish, modish and well-offish people than they, and they alone, are given the noisy, pop-infested, expensive bars they need, whether they realise it or not.

It is an approach that destroys not just a nice homely building but also the essential character of the pub. A "public house" by its very definition should be open to all, regardless of age, class or income. It may, occasionally, still have two bars that mirror London's and Britain's deeply-entrenched class system, but within those walls all should be made welcome. But the old and not so old, the less rich, and the quiet and undemanding people – Londoners all – are meanly excluded from these new, garish, neon-and-plastic monstrosities.

Such change is the extreme. The fear is that it could become the norm. And meanwhile the brewers are nibbling away even at buildings that nominally remain as "pubs". Again the aim is to pack in the traffic, and traffic that is noticeably well-heeled but older than the rock-and-lager youngsters of the café bars. Pubs for this group need a bit of "tradition", even if that tradition is confined to polystyrene beams, fake log fires, pot plants in every plastic niche, books by the yard bought as job lots in jumble sales, micro-waved "perfect portion" food from a deep freeze ... and prices that deter even those on middle incomes. The result is the same as with a Dôme or a Drummonds; the folk who look upon the pub as their "local" are made to feel unwelcome and unwanted. They get the message and vote with their feet.

MISSING EMPRESS

A pub that should have been in this book has been prevented from making an appearance by Whitbread, one of the brewing giants. The Empress of Russia in St John Street, Finsbury, EC1, was a long-time favourite of mine and, more important, of many people who live and work in the area. Although it is not the pub nearest to Sadler's Wells Theatre it was used by the members of the orchestra. There is a useful rule of thumb in London's theatre-land: if you want to know the best pub, follow the band.

The Empress was a large, two-bar pub with a folk club in an upstairs room. It was slightly faded, the lino was a bit cracked and it needed a dab of paint here and there, but it was a homely place, serving excellent ale and simple food. I would often see Aubrey, the licensee, returning from his shopping with a basket of freshly-baked French bread, a Stilton cheese and some ham just cut from the bone. Lunch in the Empress was basic, filling and remarkably good value; seventy pence for Stilton, ninety pence for a great plate of ham.

The back bar had a large television set and was popular with pensioners from the surrounding council estates who would watch their favourite soaps as they lingered over a Guinness. The front bar was busy at lunchtimes with people from the theatre and local offices; it was often packed in the evenings, especially when the folk club was going full bore upstairs. Then Aubrey retired and the brewery decided to put an end to this populist nonsense. The Empress was closed for several weeks and the dreaded tart-up teams moved in.

When it re-opened it did not look much different from the outside but the interior was changed, all changed. Like re-born zealots of some fanatical religious clan, the brewery had decided that the Empress must at all costs be a one-bar pub, even though the structure of the place made this a nonsense. They had ripped out the old bar and put in a new one that runs parallel to the street. The effect is grotesque: there are still two rooms, linked by a narrow passageway in front of the bar.

The place is decked out with dinky little lights, wall prints of Russian advertisements and newspaper cuttings of old Russian events (replacing the old and fascinating Sadler's Wells theatre bills), and the folk club has been banished. A new food servery with a sign announcing "home made food" (whose home, I wonder) has the

A glass of "whaite waine" in the revamped Empress of Russia

standard, unimaginative quiche, pies and pasties with a minute portion of Stilton that would give Aubrey apoplexy.

The clientele is now made up of transient business people in smart clothes, who tend to drink gin and tonic rather than ale. The old folk don't come around much any more, but the brewers are happy because profits have increased.

THREAT TO BEER

This violation of London's pubs is matched by the assault on the beer they serve. When even the bigger brewers were regional companies, they kept in tune with their customers and their publicans. They produced regional beers to suit regional tastes. Then, in a rush in the nineteen-sixties and seventies, six regional brewers transformed themselves into national combines and set off down the road of "national brands", producing pressurised beers and lagers with as much character and taste as an empty space. Lager, an insipid caricature of the fine beers brewed in Germany, the Netherlands, Czechoslovakia and other countries that pioneered "bottom fermentation" brewing, is immensely profitable for the beer giants, promoted with sleazy brilliance at a gullible young market.

In its bubbly wake, many fine regional beers have been phased out. Even some of the "real ales" produced by the national groups are little better than some of their ersatz lagers. Bland, identikit, designed to appeal to the lowest common denominator, they lack those strong, earthy, local tastes that the smaller companies fortunately are still able to capture in their fine ales. The likes of Webster's Yorkshire Bitter (from the Watney stable), Flowers IPA (from Whitbread) or Taylor Walker Best Bitter (from Allied Breweries) are not exactly the taste sensations of the decade.

It may seem perverse that so many of the pubs in this guide belong to two relatively small breweries, Fullers and Youngs, London's remaining independents. But they are close to their customers – the chairman of Youngs visits all his pubs on a regular basis and knows his licensees by name – and continue to provide tasty, wholehearted ales in public houses that are still worthy of the name.

This guide is a pointer towards pleasure. The aim is to present a list of pubs that you will go to, and return to, with undiminished enjoyment. But CAMRA and I would be failing in our duty if we did not underscore the appalling things being done to many of our pubs and our beers. Will many of the pubs listed here still be around in five or ten years time or will they too have been turned into plastic "profit centres" for the passing "traffic"?

The challenge to preserve our pubs and our beers is one that CAMRA is happy to accept. We need your support. But first you must decide if the pubs and beers are worthy of protection. Go forth and savour them. And if you like them, add your voice to the growing clamour for their survival.

Roger Protz

HOW TO USE THIS GUIDE

London has been divided into several areas, beginning with the two central areas, the West End, based around the great shopping thoroughfares and the theatres, and the City, the commercial area. It then follows, in geographic order, the outlying suburbs of East, North, South and West London. North London is divided into the North and North West postal districts, South London similarly into South East and South West. Places on the fringes of London that have no postal numbers, such as Croydon, Richmond and Twickenham, appear at the end of their relevant sections.

GETTING AROUND IN LONDON

The guide lists London Underground and British Rail stations for each pub. Bus routes are not shown because of the sheer volume of numbers and the fact that routes are frequently changed. Visitors to London are recommended to obtain bus and underground maps from London Underground stations and bus garages and one of the many street gazeteers to supplement the maps provided. Except in outlying areas, driving and parking are impossible ... and also undesirable if you are planning to drink. The Underground is not always reliable but it is the most effective way of getting around. Walking, of course, is a healthy alternative in the central areas and does allow you to see other attractions in between the pubs.

HOW TO SURVIVE IN THE LONDON PUB

This advice is aimed primarily at visitors from abroad. Britain, unlike most other countries, serves most of its beer in draught form rather than in bottles, which means that most beer is consumed in pubs. Do not just ask for "a beer", a meaningless request in London. Every pub will have at least one bitter, plus stout and lager on the bar, with a wide range of bottled beers behind it (British beer is explained in the next section). Bitter often comes in two forms – ordinary bitter and best or special bitter. Best and special are stronger. You must ask specifically for the beer you want i.e. a pint of bitter. In London real ale is nearly always served by a handpump, a tall lever on the bar with a clip giving the name of each brand. Don't be afraid to ask for help or even to point at the brand you want, but you must specify the quantity required: a half pint or a pint.

There are two kinds of pubs: a tied house, which means it is owned directly by the brewery and may sell only that brewery's products (guest beers from other companies are sometimes allowed); and a free house, which means it is run by someone independent of the brewery groups and serves a wide range of beer. (A number of free houses in the guide are actually owned by subsidiaries of large brewers, such as Nicholson's Inns, part of Allied Brewers, but they do offer a wider range than a normal tied pub.)

In a tied pub, it is usually sufficient to just ask for a "pint of bitter" or whatever you fancy; in a free house you must be more specific. For example, in a pub owned by Young's just ask for bitter or special. If those beers are on sale in a free house, you would have to name the brewery – "A pint of Young's bitter, please", – as there will be several other bitters on sale.

You have to pay for your beer when you order it. There is no equivalent of the French bar system where you keep your tickets and pay when you leave.

When food is described as "good" or "imaginative" that means that it is considered to be good by **general pub standards**. Pub food should not be compared to restaurant fare; it is not necessarily worse, just different, aimed at people who want a quick meal with a drink. For greater detail of pub food in London, see our companion book, the Good Pub Food Guide.

Please refer to the following sections for information about pub opening times and when children are allowed into pubs.

WHAT IS REAL ALE?

Real ale is a definition accepted by the Concise Oxford Dictionary. It is also known as traditional draught beer or cask-conditioned beer. Real ale is brewed from malted barley, using pure water and hops, and fermented by top-fermenting yeast. At the end of fermentation the beer is allowed to condition for a few days and is then racked into casks, often with the addition of priming sugar and a handful of dry hops for aroma. The beer continues to "work" or ferment in the cask while a clearing agent called finings drags the yeasty deposits to the floor of the cask. The beer is neither filtered nor pasteurised and must not be served by any method using applied gas pressure.

Real ale can be served straight from the cask and many country pubs still use this method, while some special winter brews in town pubs are often dispensed from a cask on the bar. But most real ale is drawn – hence the word "draught" – by a suction pump from the pub cellar. The pump is operated either by a handpump, a tall lever on the bar, or by an electric pump. Electric pumps are rare in the south of England but are used widely in the Midlands and the North.

Real ale should be served at a temperature of 55–56 degrees F (12–13 degrees C). This is a cool temperature that brings out the best characteristics of a top-fermented beer. It is a higher temperature than those used for serving lager beers, but it is pure mythology that real ale is "warm".

PUB HOURS

In August 1988 the British Government made long-overdue changes to pub licensing laws, which had been severely restricted since the First World War. Pubs can now open Monday to Saturday from 11 am until 11 pm. But individual licensees can choose which hours they wish to open between 11 in the morning and 11 at night. They will choose their hours to suit their trade. Many pubs now display their opening hours on the exterior. The changes came too late to monitor their effect for this guide but it is likely that pubs in tourist areas or areas of high urban concentration will stay open in the afternoon, especially in the summer. During the winter months it is likely that many pubs will keep to the old hours and will close between 3 pm and 5.30 or 6 pm. Sunday hours have been only slightly extended: the standard hours are 12 noon to 3 pm and 7 pm to 10.30 pm.

CHILDREN IN PUBS

You cannot drink alcohol in a pub below the age of eighteen years (although at sixteen, children with adults may drink beer, wine or cider with a meal). You can go into a pub at fourteen but you can drink only non-alcoholic products. Licensees their licences to trade. Children of all ages can go into pubs that have rooms set aside as "family rooms". They can also eat in pubs that have rooms used as restaurants. If a pub in this guide is shown to have a beer garden then children can use this facility but if the garden is reached via the pub it is wise for parents or guardians to ask permission to take the children through the licensed area.

SYMBOLS

The practical information for each pub is given in the form of symbols as shown below:

food is available as specified. This always means full meals unless otherwise indicated. Many pubs do not serve meals late in the evening, so check by phone if you wish to eat late.

a garden, or where specified, other outdoor area for drinking – occasionally this will just be tables on the pavement.

a family room or area without a bar is provided where the licensee will allow children accompanied by a parent or other responsible adult. In pubs where meals are served, children may be confined to the dining area, and thus be expected to have a meal. Check with staff.

the type of accommodation is specified, but no prices are given. Check by phone for availability.

real ales are listed with beers from independent breweries and national brands. For full details of local beers see the brewery section on p 25 or consult CAMRA's Good Beer Guide.

nearest Underground station. This will be just a few minutes' walk unless otherwise stated.

nearest British Rail station.

frequent live entertainment, either theatre or music.

THE STORY OF LONDON BEER

London for centuries was one of the great brewing capitals and its products were acclaimed throughout the world. When the Archbishop of Canterbury, Thomas à Becket, took two chariot loads of ale on a diplomatic mission to France in 1158 the beverage was described as being "decocted from choice fat grain as a gift for the French who wondered at such an invention – a drink most wholesome, clear of all dregs, rivalling wine in colour and surpassing it in savour". That beer was almost certainly brewed in London or nearby Hertfordshire – when Becket was a lowly priest in Hertfordshire one of his tasks was to brew ale for the monks of St Albans Abbey – and in the centuries that followed London beer was in great demand in both Europe, North America and the British colonies.

And yet today London has been reduced to just a handful of breweries. Such famous and historic names in London brewing as Charrington, Courage and Whitbread have long since left the capital. Watney's giant brewery on the Thames at Mortlake concentrates on lager and brews not a single drop of traditional draught British beer, while its subsidiary Truman in East London is down to just one traditional beer and there are doubts about the future of the plant. Guinness in West London concentrates on brewing pressurised stout and, again, there are doubts about the long-term future of its bottled stout, which, like Champagne, produces a secondary fermentation in the bottle.

The only fervent brewers of traditional beer in London are the two independents, Youngs and Fullers, together with the tiny Pitfield Brewery in Hackney, which owns just one pub. In brewing terms, London has been reduced from a capital to a suburb.

It was not always the case. In the eleventh century the Domesday Book recorded that the monks of St Paul's Cathedral brewed annually some 67,000 gallons of ale. When brewing spread from the monasteries into the town, all alehouses produced their own ale. But the demands of a growing populace soon gave rise to commercial or "common" brewers, who were not confined to a single alehouse. A Brewers' Company was set up in 1437 to represent the interests of commercial brewers and the company was given a new charter by Queen Elizabeth I in 1560 when there were twenty-six commercial brewers operating in London.

Although there was a plentiful supply of fresh well water in the capital, many of the commercial breweries were established alongside the Thames, where the water was used for brewing and the river was subsequently called upon to transport the finished products by barge and ship. River water was considered particularly good for producing the dark beer popular in London. The water was boiled, of course, during the brewing process but it is neverthless a daunting thought that river water was being used by mighty breweries such as Courage and Barclay Perkins in the eighteenth and nineteenth centuries at a time when sittings of the Houses of Parliament had to be suspended because of the appalling stench from the ordure-laden Thames.

By the end of the seventeenth century there were close to 200 commercial brewers in London. The increase had been fuelled in part by the switch from unhopped, heavy and sweet ale to the lighter and more bitter hopped beer which followed the arrival of the hop plant in southern England from the Low Countries. Commercial brewing was given greater impetus by the spread of new technologies, such as coal power, which were beyond the means of alehouse brewers, and the development of a beer style known as porter, which became so popular in London and its environs that only large commercial concerns could meet the insatiable demand.

In the early eighteenth century such famous names as Truman and Whitbread had established large breweries in the capital. They were to be followed by Charrington, Ind, Courage, Barclay, Perkins, Thrale and later by Watney and soon all were making fortunes from porter.

According to legend porter was invented in 1722 by Ralph Harwood, owner of the Bell Brewhouse in Shoreditch. A popular beer of the time was a mixture of pale, young brown ale and "stale" (mature) brown ale, known as three threads, probably a corruption of three thirds. In the days before engines pumped beer to the bar, potboys had to go to the cellars to fill drinkers' mugs from three different casks or butts. Harwood hit upon the idea of brewing one beer that would taste like three threads. The result was a dark brown beer called "entire butt" which became so popular with street and market porters that it rapidly became known by the title of porter. The strongest type of porter was called stout, not then because of its colour but simply because it was the stoutest beer produced in a brewery.

The new commercial brewers rushed to meet the demand and built large brewhouses designed only to produce porter. By 1812 Samuel Whitbread's brewery at Chiswell Street, using steam power, was churning out 122,000 barrels of porter a year, while Barclay Perkins produced 270,000, Meux Reid 188,000 and Truman Hanbury 150,000. When Henry Thrale opened his new porter vat, a hundred people sat down to dine in it. His competitors hurried to outdo him

Samuel Whitbread's porter brewery in Chiswell Street

with even larger vats and this absurd behaviour was curbed only when a porter vat at the Horse Shoe Brewery in Tottenham Court Road (on the spot where the Dominion Theatre now stands) burst in 1814. The beery deluge swept away brewery walls and other buildings and eight people were drowned.

Porter's supremacy was challenged with the emergence of Burton upon Trent as a major brewing centre. The high deposits of gypsum in the Burton water made it possible to brew a lighter coloured beer, which, heavily hopped, had good keeping qualities and could withstand long journeys to the colonies. India Pale Ale, as bitter beer was first called, soon became popular in Britain, too, and that popularity was heightened by the mass production of glass: drinkers could now see what they were drinking and they

Meux's Horseshoe Brewery, Tottenham Court Road

demanded beer that was clear in colour and free of dregs. The London brewers either set up breweries in Burton to produce bitter or learned to treat the softer London water with gypsum salts.

Bitter, Britain's unique contribution to the world of beer, was the catalyst for the great modern brewing industry centred in London and Burton. It was only when the London brewers turned their backs on bitter and were suborned in the late 1970s by the quick and easy profits from a fake Euro beer called lager that the capital went into a rapid decline as a brewing centre. Now "national branding" is the trumpet call of the marketing departments, and breweries have to be placed close to motorways in order to trunk identikit "lagerades" to all parts of the country.

The decline of London is the result of simple greed and a woeful lack of pride in British beer. It would be unthinkable for the great brewers of Munich, or Pilsen, or Copenhagen to abandon their birthright and transfer most of their production to an insipid version of a foreign beer. Distressingly, that is what so many of the great London brewers have done, which is why it is imperative to support those who have kept their Cockney roots and continue to brew the top-fermented bitters that were once the envy of the world.

(For a fuller history of British brewing see the author's Great British Beer Book, available from CAMRA, £5.95.)

REAL ALE IN LONDON

The following commercial breweries produce cask-conditioned real ale in London. (Original Gravity – OG – refers to the measurement of the fermentable material present in a brew on which excise duty is paid: it is a good indication of the strength of each beer.)

FULLER, SMITH AND TURNER of Chiswick

An old established company, Fullers have been brewing at the Griffin Brewery since 1664. Their beers have won many prizes and ESB (Extra Special Bitter) has frequently been named Champion Beer of Britain at CAMRA's annual Great British Beer Festival.
CHISWICK BITTER (OG 1035): a light, fruity, quenching bitter with a good hop character and long, bitter finish
LONDON PRIDE (OG 1041.5): a superb blend of malt and hops, an amazingly complex beer full of subtle fruity undertones
EXTRA SPECIAL BITTER (OG 1055.75): an explosion of malt and hops, strong yet rounded and not sweet, a classic strong English bitter

ARTHUR GUINNESS & SONS

Park Royal is the London base of the Dublin company established in 1759. "Draught" Guinness Stout is a pressurised beer.
GUINNESS EXTRA STOUT (OG 1042): a superb jet-black bottled beer using roasted barley as well as barley malt and a high hop level. A brilliant bitter-sweet palate. The version found in pubs is conditioned in the bottle; the version found in supermarkets and off-licences is pasteurised.

PITFIELD BREWERY of Hoxton

This young company was set up in 1981 by Rob Jones and Martin Kemp who had been running the Beer Shop in Pitfield Street for several years.

They supply the free trade and acquired their first pub in 1988. In 1987 their Dark Star beer won the Supreme Champion Beer of Britain award at the Great British Beer Festival.

PITFIELD BITTER (OG 1038): a nutty flavoured, copper-coloured beer, malty and distinctive.

HOXTON SPECIAL (OG 1048): a well-rounded, well-crafted ale with a malty sweetness offset by generous hopping.

DARK STAR (OG 1050): a beer similar in style to an old London porter, full of good malt flavour, with chocolate and raisin undertones and a long, dry finish.

TRUMAN of Brick Lane, Whitechapel

One of London's oldest breweries, due to be closed by Watney/Grand Metropolitan in 1989 when beer production will be switched to Wiltshire.

TRUMAN BEST BITTER (OG 1045): A typical Big Brewery beer, professionally made, with an appealing nose but disappointingly bland for its gravity, probably due to the use of unmalted adjuncts.

YOUNG & CO of Wandsworth

Youngs have been brewing at the Ram Brewery since 1831. The company is wedded to traditional values, refused to join the great swing to keg beer in the 1970s and, while it now produces its own lager brands, enthusiastically supports its cask beers which are delivered to some outlets by horse-drawn drays.

BITTER (OG 1036): a classic London bitter, fruity yet intensely hoppy with a brilliant finish — always called "Ordinary" in Young's pubs, a curious misnomer.

SPECIAL BITTER (OG 1046): a brilliantly crafted beer with a pronounced orange peel nose and a wonderful balance between malt and hops; an exceptionally hoppy edge for a beer of its gravity.

WINTER WARMER (OG 1055): a winter brew, a

rich and ripe old ale, with a sharp prickle of hops behind the smooth maltiness.

For details of all other beers on sale in London pubs, see the CAMRA Good Beer Guide, which lists every draught beer brewed in Britain with their original gravities. The guide also lists home-brew pubs based in London.

Hermit hoar, in solemn cell,
    Wearing out life's evening gray;
Strike thy bosom, Sage! and tell
What is bliss, and which the way?
Thus I spoke, and speaking sigh'd
Scarce repress'd the starting tear,
When the hoary Sage reply'd,
'Come, my lad, and drink some beer.'
Dr Samuel Johnson

CENTRAL LONDON
THE WEST END

WI
Argyll Arms

18 Argyll Street

✖ lunchtime and evening

🍺 **Adnams Bitter; Boddingtons Bitter; Tetley Bitter; Wadworth 6X**

The Argyll is one of London's finest Victorian public houses, a riot of engraved glass partitions and giant mirrors, with the intimate feel of its period kept intact by preserving the original bars. Nicholson's Inns, who acquired the pub from Bass, deserve praise for refusing to indulge in the vulgar modern practice of knocking any existing pub with several bars into one large and impersonal room.

The pub was built in 1868 but there has been a tavern on the site since the turn of the seventeenth century. The present building has a preservation order placed on it and is named after the noble Scottish family. The Duke of Argyll's London residence was a mansion on the site of London's most famous music hall, the London Palladium, a few yards from the pub. The Argyll's influence was clearly powerful in the area and probably influenced the nearby Clachan pub in Kingly Street (see entry).

The tall, narrow building has four storeys. The pavement outside, opposite an exit from the Underground station, has been turned into a pedestrian precinct. On pleasant days, the crowds that pack into the Argyll spill on to the pavement to talk and to enjoy their drinks. Inside the bars – saloon, public, private and ladies' – are divided by glass partitions.

The three front bars are tiny, the back room vast and imposing. There are pot plants in handsome holders, a stunning stucco ceiling and a splendid example of a nineteenth century Bass mirror. Mahogany cabinets are the work of master craftsmen and one of the most fascinating artefacts is the old manager's pulpit-like tiny office in the middle of the pub, from which he could keep an eye on all the bars. Even the "gents" are a work of art – I cannot vouch for the ladies, but have no doubt that they follow suit.

There are good hot lunches and evening

snacks. Salt beef sandwiches are the house speciality. Children of all ages should note that a short walk away in Regent's Street is Hamley's, the world-famous, multi-storeyed toy shop with delights on every floor.

⊖ Oxford Circus

Places to see: Oxford Street, Regent's Street

Clachan

34 Kingly Street

✗ lunchtime and evening

🍺 **Adnams Bitter; Boddingtons Bitter; Tetley Bitter; Wadworth 6X; Friary Meux Best Bitter**

Clachan is Gaelic for a small village but there is nothing rural about this large pub a few yards from Carnaby Street, which is now a rather tatty and faded echo of its Swinging Sixties hippy glory. The only touch of the Highlands in the pub is in the raised section at the back of the large bar, where an unusual glass roof has stained glass paintings of Scottish soldiers in Highland dress.

The Clachan, with a panelled frontage and its name picked out in huge gilt letters, has been lavishly restored by Nicholson's Inns. Inside there is a painted stucco ceiling, engraved glass partitions, old prints on the walls, stools and sofas, and a mass of pot plants. A vast circular bar, with a built-in food servery, dominates the pub and divides it into a series of intimate areas. Light streams in through the panelled windows that overlook Kingly Street.

Food is served lunchtime and evening and offers a wide range of hot and cold dishes. You may find steak and kidney pie, sausages in French bread, quiche, a choice of ploughman's, and filled jacket potatoes. The beer range is liable to change.

⊖ Oxford Circus/Piccadilly Circus

Places to see: Regent's Street, Carnaby Street, Piccadilly Circus

De Hems

Macclesfield Street

✕ lunchtime and evening

▣ **Adnams Bitter; Ind Coope Burton Ale; Taylor Walker Best Bitter**

De Hems – the windmill – is a Dutch-style bar in the heart of Chinatown. Macclesfield Street, just a few yards' long, runs between Gerrard Street, knee-deep in chop sticks and Soy sauce, and Shaftesbury Avenue. Chinatown has been brilliantly transformed in recent years from a seedy area into a vibrant one packed with pagodas, engaging Chinese chatter and excellent restaurants and food shops, spoiled only by a few porno cinemas. The streets, including Macclesfield Street, have bi-lingual nameplates.

The pub is a showplace for Allied Breweries, who use it to promote their Dutch subsidiary, Oranjeboom, the Orange Tree brewery in Rotterdam. The wood-panelled walls are packed with Dutch prints, photos and pottery. Behind the small, ornate bar a mirror wishes you "Oranjeboom Gezondheit" – Bless You. There is plenty of standing room by the bar and in a large back area, and there is also a good supply of stools and wall sofas. A high ceiling and fans help to keep away nicotine fumes and on warm days the doors are folded back to open up most of the frontage.

As well as the good range of traditional British beers, an imposing porcelain "Big Bertha" fount serves original Oranjeboom beer from Rotterdam: smaller founts also serve a lager of the same name, but that is the British version, brewed in Wrexham! A good range of food – lasagne, cottage pie, beef and mushroom, chilli and ploughman's – includes special Dutch dishes such as pork saté, bitter bollen and herrings.

⊖ Piccadilly Circus/Leicester Square

Duke of Wellington

94a Crawford Street

✗ food lunchtime

▨ seats on pavement

🍺 **Charrington IPA, Draught Bass**

Not so much a pub, more a shrine to the Iron Duke. As you approach the small tavern down the wide and spacious street, you spot a caricature of him, with his head emerging from a giant Wellington boot, on the pub sign. Beneath the sign customers can sit in good weather on pavement benches. Inside the duke gives you a belligerent stare from every nook and cranny in the form of busts, effigies, portraits and cartoons. The end wall to the left by the entrance is a mass of cartoons and prints depicting the duke's campaigns. A pillar has been turned into a signpost with finger boards naming his famous European adventures and battles.

With the English devotion to fair play, the other end of the small bar has some memorabilia concerning his arch enemy, Napoleon Bonaparte. Next to a casement clock there is a large model inside a glass frame that depicts the Battle of Waterloo, complete with a Low Country windmill. A long upholstered bench runs the length of the room beneath the windows that front on to the street. Above the bench, cabinets built into the windows have China and metal figures of the duke.

Behind the tiny bar there is an old pub sign from an inn called the Iron Duke which belonged to the defunct Cobbs brewery. The Duke of Wellington has ample standing room in front of the bar, a carpeted floor and nicotine-painted moulded ceiling. Food includes a hot lunchtime special, salt beef sandwiches and toasted sandwiches.

Opposite the pub, in Wyndham Place, St. Mary's Church has an impressive frontage with a tall fluted steeple and architecture that looks more Spanish than English. You half expect the duke to clamber down from his pub sign to lead an assault on it.

⊖ Edgware Road

Places to see: St. Mary's Church, Edgware Road

George

55 Great Portland Street

✗ lunchtime and evening

🍺 **Adnams Bitter; Greene King IPA, Abbot Ale; Wadworth 6X**

This richly panelled pub with gas mantles, plump sofas and engraved mirrors is the local for people working in the headquarters of the BBC, Broadcasting House, round the corner in Portland Place. Outside, the George is charmingly decorated with hanging baskets and coach lamps. Inside, there is a vast oak bar that runs in an elegant loop all round the large saloon. The bar is surmounted by a fine gallery and there are old wine casks behind the bar as well as a collection of Toby jugs and a copy of Wisden for cricket buffs anxious to bone up on the scores from the previous season. There is plenty of seating along the bar on stools with backs.

Dylan Thomas is one of the many luminaries who have frequented the George over the years, which is known affectionately as the "Gluepot" to old BBC hands. It was given this nickname in the 1930s by the famous orchestral conductor, Sir Henry Wood, who founded the annual Promenade Concerts. He used to rehearse the BBC Symphony Orchestra in the Queen's Hall between the pub and Broadcasting House. When the players returned late and several crochets to the bar from their break he would roar "You've been drinking in that bloody Gluepot again!"

The name Gluepot is given to pubs used by factory workers in such occupations as cabinet making and furniture, and presumably the snobbish Sir Henry objected to his musicians rubbing shoulders with common working men. It is difficult to imagine anything less like a factory-gate boozer than this most elegant and beautifully-appointed tavern.

From a large servery, food, lunchtime and evenings, includes steak pie and two veg, sausage and French bread, ploughman's, and cheese, leek and ham quiche. The range of beer is likely to change.

⊖ Oxford Circus

Places to see: Oxford Street, Regent Street, Broadcasting House

Guinea

30 Bruton Place
Closed Sunday

✗ lunchtime; separate restaurant lunchtime and evening

⏴ **Young Bitter, Special Bitter, Winter Warmer**

It is difficult to believe that snooty Berkeley Square, where you can hear the nightingale sing above the purr of the Rolls-Royces, was once used as a cattle and hog pound. The Guinea, in a small mews off the square, was built in 1423 and was also known as the One Pound One, a pun on the area's former smelly claim to fame. Berkeley Square was once part of the London estate of a wealthy West Country family, the Berkeleys of Stratton, and one member of the family, Sir Maurice Berkeley of Bruton, gave his name to the mews where the pub stands. The square is now one of the smartest parts of West London and is a working and residential enclave of the well-heeled in advertising and *haute couture* and has showrooms selling cars beyond the dreams of everyday avarice.

The Guinea is a pleasingly unpretentious mews pub with a striking dormer window jutting above the ground floor. Inside the walls are decorated with Spy cartoons from *Vanity Fair* and many Victorian prints.

The narrow passageways around the dominating horseshoe bar have wooden settles and plush banquettes. The floor is carpeted and the ceiling is painted a deep ochre to soak up the worst of the nicotine. At the rear of the bar there is an imposing old wall clock close to the small servery offering hot lunchtime dishes and a wide range of filled baps.

If you go beyond the servery you suddenly find yourself in a different world. The bar is packed with cheerful drinkers enjoying a quick pint and a snack. But at the back, in sharp distinction, there is a small, intimate and smart restaurant (phone 629 5971) with a long-standing reputation for quality cooking.

⊖ Green Park

WCI
Hansler Arms

133 King's Cross Road

✖ lunchtime

🍺 **Brakspear Bitter; Whitbread Castle Eden Ale, Flowers Original; regular guest beers**

This gem of a pub is one of the smallest in London – twenty people and it is packed. It is just a few minutes' walk from the great railway stations of King's Cross and St. Pancras and yet once you are inside away from the constant roar and rumble of the main road you could be forgiven for thinking you are in a quiet suburban or rural ale house. The small frontage has a pleasant awning above the door. Inside there are old Punch cartoons and Victorian prints on the flock papered walls, a carpeted floor, pot plants in the window and small stools and tables.

The pub is on the site of an old spa named Bagnigge Wells after its founder Thomas Bagnigge (this part of London was rich in artesian wells – Sadler's Wells and Exmouth Market spa are close by). In the eighteenth century, the spa was a haunt of the rich and famous, including a Scandinavian diplomat named Joseph Hansler. He became a British citizen and had the distinction of being the first man to be knighted by Queen Victoria. A tavern was built in his honour and was a simple beer house. It did not get a full licence to serve wines and spirits until the 1960s.

This corner of central London is rich in history. Long before Mr Bagnigge built his spa, Queen Boudicca or Boadicea, the doubty fighter against the Roman empire, was finally routed there in AD62.

The Hansler Arms has a pleasing mix of customers, some of them coming from the great postal sorting office at Mount Pleasant, others from the railway stations and there is often good-natured badinage between customers and the welcoming bar staff. Food is served lunchtime and early evening and includes lasagne, moussaka, chilli and rice, beef and chicken curries, ploughman's, pies and pasties. The beer range may vary but is based on cask ales from within the Whitbread group or with breweries

🚆 King's Cross/St. Pancras

🚇 King's Cross/St. Pancras

such as Brakspear with which Whitbread has close trading ties.

Lamb

94 Lamb's Conduit Street

✗ lunchtime and evening; lunchtime restaurant

🍴 seats in courtyard

🍺 **Young Bitter, Special Bitter, Winter Warmer**

The Lamb is a sumptuous Victorian pub in the heart of the literary world of Bloomsbury, made famous between 1900 and the thirties by the "Bloomsbury Set" writers that included Leonard and Virginia Woolf, E. M. Forster, Lytton Strachey and John Maynard Keynes. The pub is in a pedestrian precinct named after a Mr Lamb who built a drain under the road. It is at one and the same time both a welcoming and an elegant drinking house, with a commanding horseshoe bar topped by snob screens. The screens are made of engraved glass and can be revolved through ninety degrees; they were installed in many nineteenth century taverns in order to allow the upper-class denizens of the saloon bar to see who was drinking in the public bar or the snug, and to close them when they did not wish to be observed carousing with members of the opposite sex to whom they were not married.

The Lamb is no longer constrained by Victorian snobbery and there is a pleasing mix of customers who stand around the bar or occupy the deeply comfortable leather chairs and benches that line the walls. The seats are fronted by small round tables with brass rails, a sensible device that prevents precious brown liquid being spilled by passers-by. The walls are packed with prints of old London and photos of many stars of the Victorian music hall.

To the left of the bar and down a couple of steps lies a wider drinking and eating area. There is also a tiny courtyard at the back where you can eat and sup, but many customers prefer to spill out into Lamb's Conduit Street itself when the weather permits. The most pleasing attribute of the Lamb is the hum of conversation. There are no juke boxes or piped music and

⊖ Russell Square

people revel in the rare opportunity to converse in a London pub without having to shout.

Food is plentiful and includes such lunchtime dishes as ham and mushroom crêpe, beef pie, chicken and mushroom pie, tortelloni and salad, quiche, chilli and rice, cauliflower cheese, fisherman's lunch and ploughman's. Lunch is also served in a large upstairs dining room. There is a cold buffet in the bar in the evening.

Mabel's

9 Mabledon Place, off Euston Road
Closed Saturday evening

✗ lunchtime and evening

🍺 seats on pavement

🍺 **Boddingtons Bitter; Brakspear Bitter; Greene King Abbot Ale; Whitbread Flowers Original, Wethered Bitter**

Mabel's is a modern pub run by Whitbread but with a good choice of beers as well as their own Flowers and Wethered. There are seats on the pavement and the frontage has engraved glass windows and hanging baskets. Inside the one large room has been cleverly divided into several smaller areas, two of them raised up from ground level by a couple of steps. The walls are partly panelled, there are lots of comfortable banquettes, carpets on the floor and more hanging baskets. The walls are decorated by old theatre and cinema prints and posters.

The lighting is soft and the food servery next to the bar offers a good range of food: fillet of plaice, scampi, quiche, lasagne, salads, ploughman's and roast gammon. Mabel's is a useful resting place for travellers using King's Cross, St. Pancras and Euston stations and is popular with the staff in the headquarters of the local government trade union NALGO.

≽ King's Cross/St. Pancras

⊖ Euston, King's Cross and St. Pancras

Pakenham Arms

1 Pakenham Street

✗ lunchtime and evening

🍺 **Boddingtons Bitter; Brakspear Special; Greene King Abbot Ale; Whitbread Flowers Original**

The Pakenham, opposite a side entrance to Mount Pleasant sorting office, is a rare find in central London, a genuine two-bar pub. As the Toby Jug logos in the windows testify, it was once a Charrington house but it has been free of the tie for many years and was a flagship for the real ale revolution in the seventies. The saloon is spacious and two-tiered, carpeted at ground level and bare-boarded on a raised area used by diners. There is an abundance of comfortable seats and sofas. The walls have marble-effect paper above lincrusta panels and are decked out with wall lights and prints of old London. The public bar is small, cheery and wood-panelled with a dartboard.

A large food cabinet in the saloon serves hot food lunchtime and evenings and may include plaice or cod and chips, steak *cordon bleu*, burgers, chicken Kiev, fisherman's basket, sausage and chips, ploughman's, and cheese and vegetarian dishes. There is a traditional roast on Sunday lunchtime. The Pakenham is popular with office workers as well as post office staff, many of whom congregate in the public bar to play darts.

The range of beer varies considerably and Adnams' and Arkells' ales often augment the ones shown above. The impressive "Big Bertha" porcelain fount in the saloon serves a genuine Bavarian beer, Hacker-Pschorr *pilsener* from Munich.

🚆 King's Cross/St. Pancras

🚇 Russell Square

Princess Louise

208 High Holborn

✗ lunchtime and evening;
separate wine bars

🍺 Boddingtons Bitter; Brakspear
Bitter, Special; Darley Thorne
Best Bitter; Greene King Abbot
Ale; Ward Sheffield Best
Bitter; Vaux Samson

As the great crowds of drinkers testify, this is one of central London's most popular pubs and one of the finest examples of Victorian pub architecture. Yet a decade ago it was dying on its feet. I remember going into the Princess Louise in the late seventies when it was a dingy and deserted Watney house. On a night of terrible humidity the lacklustre bar staff did not even have lager to offer, let alone real ale. "Sorry," I was told, "we've only got Red Barrel." No wonder Watney's infamous keg beer died a rapid death when even the brewery's employees apologised for selling it.

Soon after, the pub was sold and became a free house and eventually came under the control of the Vaux group from north east England, who still sell beers from other companies, plus a house beer, "Princess Louise Best Bitter", in honour both of the pub and the daughter of Queen Victoria, who died aged 91 and whose face appears on the pub sign. Money and care has been lavished on restoring the house to its original grandeur and more than one visit is needed to take in all the many splendours.

There is a riot of marble, Portland stone columns, etched glass windows and partitions, wood panelling, tiles, enormous etched and gilt mirrors and a crimson and gold ceiling. The windows have handsome drapes, the boards are bare and there are plenty of green plush seats and settees in the side alcoves – although it can still be difficult to find a vacant space.

The pub is enormous and is served by a vast central bar groaning with beer pumps. Bar food, which comes down an original dumb waiter, includes home-made pies, lasagne, salads and chilli con carne. There is a more extensive menu in two wine bars in the cellar and on the first floor (which stages jazz sessions at weekends).

Gentlemen visitors must visit the cavernous and palatial Victorian toilet, so impressive that it

⊖ Holborn

is the subject of a protection order in its own right.

Skinners Arms

*Corner of Judd Street and
Hastings Street*

✗ lunchtime and evening

🍴 seats on pavement

🍺 **Greene King IPA, Abbot Ale,
Rayment BBA**

Greene King, the Suffolk brewers, bought the pub a few years ago and have carefully restored a once scruffy old house that is just a couple of minutes from one of London's finest Victorian Gothic masterpieces, St. Pancras Station. Skinners is rare for the area in having two bars – and two very different bars at that. The small saloon is secluded and intimate, with small alcoves, red plush seats, claret papered walls with many Victorian prints. In sharp distinction, the large and cheerful public bar is plain, with bare floors and a large pool table.

The pub is popular with workers from both Camden Town Hall a few yards away and the nearby rail termini. Good food, in generous portions, includes a daily hot special such as roast pork and two veg, cheese and potato pie or rolls and sandwiches.

The pub is named after the Worshipful Company of Skinners, a medieval guild for fur merchants.

The one controversial note in the pub is the beer called Rayment's BBA (Best Bitter Ale). Much to the distress of beer lovers in Hertfordshire, Greene King closed the Rayment's subsidiary at Furneux Pelham in 1987 and transferred production to the main brewery in Bury St. Edmunds. Devotees say it is not the same beer, but it is still a remarkably good one and worth trying.

🚆 King's Cross/St. Pancras

🚇 King's Cross/St. Pancras

Places to see: St. Pancras
Station

White Hart

Corner of Holborn High Street and Drury Lane

✗ lunchtime and evening

🍺 **Draught Bass, Charrington IPA**

This is an ancient and historic hostelry. There has been an inn on the site since 1201 and the present Bass house, on the fringe of Covent Garden, has avoided the dreadful tart-ups that ruin too many old London pubs that ache with history. It has been left mercifully intact as a reminder of different periods when it served as a simple ale house and later as a coaching inn and tavern when Covent Garden (originally Convent Garden) was an almost rural area, the site of many grand houses – and a nunnery.

It is unlikely that the inn's original name was the White Hart, for this popular name stems from the reign of Richard II in the late fourteenth century. It was his heraldic symbol and all members of his household wore the device. Obsequious inn keepers hurried to copy them.

The half-timbered exterior of the White Hart leads into a narrow and rather unprepossessing entrance, but persevere. The long, narrow bar area opens into a large back bar with exposed beams, panelled walls and wooden side partitions.

Great globes descend from the ceiling, there are oval tables at which to eat and an enormous old fireplace with an impressive copper hood surrounded by warming pans and other utensils. It is a pity that the brewery has followed the trend of installing a mock log fire rather than leaving the real thing to blaze away naturally.

A large food servery stands against the far wall and dispenses lasagne, sweet and sour pork, chicken and chips, ploughman's and salads. The pub is a useful base for taking victuals on board before tackling the mayhem of Oxford Street and its shops.

⊖ Holborn/Covent Garden

WC 2
Chandos

29 St. Martin's Lane

✗ breakfast lunch and afternoon tea

🍺 **Samuel Smith Old Brewery Bitter, Museum Ale**

🚋 Charing Cross

⊖ Trafalgar Square

Places to see: St. Martin's in the Fields, Trafalgar Square, National Gallery

When the fiercely traditionalist Yorkshire brewers Sam Smith moved into London they bought the Chandos as one of the first of their twenty-five outlets in the capital. Vulgar modernisation is anathema to the company, whose reputation has been built on beer delivered by horse-drawn drays and served from wooden casks. The large ground-floor bar has bare boards, panelled alcoves, leather wall seats, tiled dados and leaded windows with brewery motifs.

The upstairs room has the atmosphere of a gentleman's club with deeply comfortable leather sofas, an open fire and window seats. The walls are crowded with panels that follow the history of the writing and playing of Handel's music for the royal fireworks: Lord Chandos was a patron of George Frederick Handel, the great German composer who settled in London and, later, Tunbridge Wells in Kent.

The Chandos is open all day and you can enjoy afternoon tea; breakfast is served from 8 am. Full lunches are offered in a restaurant area on the first floor while pub grub on the ground floor includes ham and garlic bake, lasagne, quiche, Cornish pastie, smoked mackerel, ploughman's and salads.

This lavishly restored tavern is ideally placed for enjoying the several delights of the area: to the left in St. Martin's Lane is the English National Opera, to the right the great sturdy edifice of St. Martin's in the Fields church and, beyond, Trafalgar Square, while the National Gallery and National Portrait Gallery are across the road.

Cittie of York

22 High Holborn
Closed Sunday

✘ lunchtime and evening

🍺 **Samuel Smith Old Brewery Bitter, Museum Ale**

This enormous old drinking hall with its great vaulted roof is more like a gothic palace than a pub. It is popular with lawyers and judges from the Law Courts and the Inns of Court off Gray's Inn Road. It was a celebrated Henekey's wine-only tavern for a century or more until it was bought by Sam Smith of Tadcaster when the Yorkshire firm made its calculated assault on London with a string of tied houses. The Yorkshire connection is stressed as you enter the hall from the street, with medieval painted panels and plaster versions of the White Rose of York. This takes you into the main bar, with the longest counter in Britain, surmounted by a gantry carrying old wine butts that each contained a thousand gallons. There is a catwalk above the butts, used by staff who once had the onerous task of refilling the casks – they were drained of their contents during the Second World War "Blitz" on London.

Large lamps are suspended from the high raftered ceiling and the room is heated by a fierce and efficient triangular coal-fired stove. Opposite the counter and running the length of the room is a series of side cubicles with intricate carvings, tables and an intimate atmosphere.

A smaller wood-panelled room off the main hall has brass lights and a mass of prints of old York. Lunchtime food is served in the main bar and in the downstairs Barnaby Rudge room (another Dickens connection!) and includes pasta Bolognaise, cauliflower cheese, chicken nuggets and ploughman's.

⊖ Chancery Lane

George

213 Strand
Closed Sunday evening

✖ lunchtime and evening;
separate restaurant

🍺 **Draught Bass, Charrington
IPA**

The George, a tall and imposing timber-framed building standing opposite the great façade of the Law Courts, marks where Fleet Street ends and the Strand begins. Walk through the narrow oak doors into the vast long bar and you are in the genuine atmosphere of an eighteenth-century coffee house where the intellectuals and dandies of those days congregated to talk, denounce the government and plan and raise the finance for their pamphlets and satirical magazines. Today it is the haunt of lawyers and barristers, many of them still in their working clothes of wigs and gowns, who drop in for lunch from either the court or their offices in the Inns of Court — some of London's finest buildings that lie behind the George and run down to the Embankment.

The inn, carefully restored by Bass in recent years, shows King George III on the pub sign but was originally named after a landlord called George. It has bare boards, a beamed ceiling, side alcoves and benches and an enormous wood and pillared bar running almost the whole length of the building. There is a side entrance in an alleyway and a spacious area to the rear of the main bar with a food servery offering quiche Lorraine, scotch eggs, roll mops, smoked mackerel and ploughmans.

Between the servery and the bar, a door and narrow stairs lead up to a delightful dining room with fine views of the Law Courts from the latticed windows.

To the left of the George, amid the mad hurly-burly of the traffic, stands the serene church of St. Clements Dane, slap in the middle of the Strand. "The bells of St Clements" feature in a famous old London song about London churches; the "Dane" is thought to refer to a Danish settlement on the site in the time of King Canute. Outside the church is a statue of Dr

⊖ Temple

Samuel Johnson, a great frequenter of taverns in the area.

Marquess of Anglesey

39 Bow Street

✗ lunchtime and evening; separate restaurant

🍺 **Young Bitter, Special Bitter, Winter Warmer**

The demand for Young's beer in the Marquess is so insatiable that the brewery has had to extend what was once a small street-corner local into larger premises. It stands in the heart of Covent Garden, close to the Royal Opera House and Drury Lane Theatre and in the street with a world-famous "nick" or police station which gave the name to the special squad of policemen known as the Bow Street Runners. Covent Garden was once a major market but it has long since moved away from the congestion of central London and the planners have for once produced something of quality in the modern capital.

The area has been brilliantly transformed into an open-air and partially-covered Italianate piazza with street cafés and book shops. As you stroll towards the pub you may find impromptu street performances of Vivaldi and Paraguayan music on native flutes, while a juggler practises his art in front of his windowed reflection.

The Marquess has an elegant pebbled glass interior that leads into a cheery saloon with a large horseshoe bar with a few tables and chairs. To the left and up one step there is the charming new seating area so cleverly designed that it manages to be both large and intimate at the same time. There are comfortable plush chairs and sofas, pretty flowered wallpaper and matching curtains and drapes.

A collection of china dishes has pride of place on a shelf on the far wall and there are many prints of old London and a forbidding portrait of a beetle-browed gentleman decked out with military medals and a heavy mayoral chain. The pub has an extensive range of food, chalked on a board on the pavement, and offers T-bone steaks, lamb in claret, grilled plaice, *chilli con carne, ratatouille,* steak and kidney pie and lamb curry. Food can be eaten in the bar or in an upstairs restaurant.

Covent Garden has many delights. As well as the theatres and the *al fresco* performances, don't miss the chance to visit the fascinating London Transport Museum, which traces the history of public transport in the capital and recalls an age when buses, tubes, trams and trolley cars provided a splendid, cheap and reliable service.

◒ Covent Garden

Places to see: The piazza, Royal Opera House, Drury Lane Theatre, Transport Museum

Lamb and Flag

33 Rose Street

✖ hot lunches and evening snacks

🍺 **Courage Best Bitter, Directors Bitter, John Smith Yorkshire Bitter**

Yet another London pub frequented by Charles Dickens and little has changed since his days in the large wood-panelled back room with an open fire and high-backed settles. It is the oldest wooden-framed Tudor pub still surviving in the capital and it has been licensed since 1623. As you approach the pub, with mullioned windows and a large coaching lamp over the entrance in a side alley, the door to the left opens into a tiny front bar, often so packed that drinkers are forced to take up a curious posture of raising their drinking arms above their heads in order not to spill precious liquid as they converse. The main bar is reached down the alley; the entrance takes you into a tiny panelled passageway alongside the bar, which opens into the large back room.

The upstairs Dryden Room is used as a lunchtime restaurant and as an overspill bar in the evening. The whole building is crowded with old prints of the Restoration period. The Dryden Room is named in honour of the poet John Dryden who was almost killed in the alleyway in 1679 when he was ambushed by a gang hired by Louise de Keroualle, the mistress of King Charles

II. A notice in Rose Alley gives details of the attack and there are old newspaper cuttings about it in the back bar.

The pub did have an unsavoury reputation for many years. Its original name was the Cooper's Arms but it was known throughout the Covent Garden area as the Bucket of Blood as bare-knuckle prize fights were staged in the upstairs room. The present name is a religious and heraldic one: the lamb refers to the son of God and was used as the device of the Knights Templar and the Merchant Tailors company.

The attempt on Dryden's life is commemorated in the Lamb and Flag every December 19 when the landlord serves free glasses of mulled ale – hot beer with spices – or sack posset, a concoction of sherry, sugar and spices in hot milk. I would stick to Courage Best if I were you.

Excellent lunchtime meals in the pub include *duck à l'orange*, beef and mushrooms, chilli, turkey baps and filled jacket potatoes.

⊖ Leicester Square and Covent Garden

Places to see: Charing Cross Road, Covent Garden

Nag's Head

Corner of James Street and Floral Street
Closed Sunday evening

✘ lunchtime

🍺 **McMullen AK Mild, Country Bitter, Christmas Ale**

This splendidly ornate watering hole, just a few yards from the splendours of Inigo Jones's Palladian Covent Garden and the Royal Opera House, is the London flagship of the country brewers McMullen of Hertford. They are one of the few southern brewers who still brew a mild ale, though AK is more of a light bitter than a genuine mild. Both AK and the stronger Country Bitter are deliciously nutty, tangy beers.

The large glazed windows have the name "McMullen of Hertford" engraved on them. Inside a large horseshoe bar is surmounted by a canopy with leaded lights and old brandy and gin casks on the top. Large lamps and fans are suspended from the ochre-coloured ceiling. The large room, with an attractive pale wallpaper, is divided by a number of partitions to give a feeling of intimacy and there is an abundance of comfortable bench seats.

There is additional seating and standing room beyond the sweep of the bar and a servery offers such dishes as meat and potato pie, shepherd's pie, chilli and ploughman's.

The pub sign shows a circus pony. "Nag" is a colloquialism for a small horse but it has a double meaning, for pestering wives are also known as nags. Some Nag's Head pubs have signs showing the scowling faces of women or even a woman wearing a muzzle. But McMullen know better than to upset the liberated ladies of central London and have wisely stuck to tradition.

⊖ Covent Garden

Places to see: Covent Garden, Royal Opera House

Opera Tavern

23 Catherine Street
Closed Sunday

✘ lunchtime and evening; separate restaurant

🍽 seats on pavement

🍺 **Benskins Best Bitter, Ind Coope Burton Ale, Taylor Walker Best Bitter**

This charming old pub stands opposite the Theatre Royal, Drury Lane, not the Royal Opera House – but, to add to the confusion, the Theatre Royal began life as an opera house, so the pub's name is apt. It has a strikingly bold and colourful frontage with two small windows jutting over the pavement, which has a few tables and chairs for warm weather.

The tavern was built in 1879 by the architect John Treacher who specialised in pub design. Inside the wood-panelled walls are crowded with old play bills and photographs of stars past and present who have appeared at the Theatre Royal.

There are plenty of bar stools as well as seats built into the walls. The floor is carpeted and fans (the cooling type, not theatregoers) are suspended from the ceiling. The centrepiece of the tavern is the superb mirrored and panelled wall behind the bar. To the right of the bar a servery dishes up a splendid range of tasty food, including tuna savoury, Cumberland sausage, salmon and dill quiche, vegetarian Cornish pastie, ploughman's and gooseberry crumble.

⊖ Covent Garden

Sherlock Holmes

*10 Northumberland Avenue
(corner of Craven Passage)*

✘ lunchtime and evening;
separate restaurant

🍴 seats on pavement

🍺 **Boddingtons Bitter; Brakspear Bitter; Greene King Abbot Ale; Whitbread Flowers Original**

I have known and loved this wonderful pub since it was my local when I was a National Serviceman stationed across the road in the War (sic) Office. This Whitbread inn, now run as a free house, was a "theme pub" long before other brewers devalued the coinage. It is a shrine to the great detective and to his creator: Sir Arthur Conan Doyle's face and name are engraved in the windows. Inside there is a plethora of playbills, and cinema and television stills depicting various actors that have played Holmes and Dr Watson over the decades, including the incomparable Basil Rathbone. There is also a violin case, an awesome head of the Baskerville hound and a cabinet packed with Victorian police whistles, poison bottles, a magnifying glass, extracts from the novels and a picture of the long-suffering landlady of 221B Baker Street, Mrs Hudson.

Mrs Hudson's name also appears above the food "pantry" (fortunately the owners stopped short of naming the toilets the Reichenbach Falls) which offers macaroni cheese – a favourite of Moriarty's – steak and kidney pie, lasagne, shepherd's pie, quiche and salad, and ploughman's.

A restaurant on the first floor has been brilliantly designed as Holmes's study in Baker Street, with booklined walls and a model of the detective himself.

In case you'd forgotten, it *is* a pub. There are wall seats, stools, tables, a carpeted floor and electric versions of gas mantles.

Now, if you are wondering why a pub devoted to Sherlock Holmes is situated so far from Baker Street, then you are not a true Conan Doyle buff. As all real devotees will immediately tell you, it was in the Northumberland Hotel (now the War Office) that Holmes first met Sir Henry Baskerville.

🚂 Charing Cross

⊖ Embankment/Trafalgar Square

Places to see: Trafalgar Square

THE CITY
INCLUDING FINSBURY
AND FLEET STREET

EC1
Castle

34/35 Cowcross Street
Closed Sunday

✗ lunchtime

🍺 **Draught Bass, Charrington IPA**

🚆 Farringdon

⊖ Farringdon

Places to see: Smithfield Market

*"To pop", in London parlance, is the act of exchanging a valuable for money in a pawnbroker's

If you run short of the readies, the Castle could be your salvation, for it is London's only licensed pawnbroker. It owes this curious distinction to the occasion in the 1830s when the profligate and wayward King George IV lost his money gambling at a cock fight. Fancying a swift one on the way home, he popped (if you'll pardon the pun*) into the Castle and asked the inn keeper for a small loan. He left his watch as security and a court official returned a few days later to retrieve the time piece. As a result, the landlord was granted a licence to act as a pawnbroker as well as a publican: a large painting on the left-hand wall commemorates the granting of the licence.

Above the bar opposite is the traditional sign of the pawnbroker: three balls, which you may think sums up the pub's legend. You are unlikely, however, to get cash in exchange for a valuable and the bar staff will probably good naturedly point you in the direction of the nearest "Uncle's", as Londoners call a pawnbroker.

The Castle is on the edge of the capital's great meat market, Smithfield, attracting both market workers in their blood-stained clothes and smart City gents in their neat suits. The pub has been considerably changed and up-graded by Bass, though the fake gas mantles and mass of old prints of London mix somewhat incongruously with an impressive original Wurlitzer juke box which stands below the oil painting. There is a superb old Bass mirror and a small seating area at the rear. The pub serves hot lunches, and rolls, sandwiches and quiche in the evening.

Crown Tavern

43 Clerkenwell Green
Closed Sunday

✗ lunchtime; separate
restaurant

⊕ seats on pavement

⊟ **Adnams Bitter; Boddingtons
Bitter; Wadworth 6X; Ind
Coope Burton Ale, Tetley
Bitter**

Clerkenwell Green, once a boisterous area of republican, radical and trade union activity, is now a lively small business area, framed by elegant houses that include the headquarters of the London Philharmonic Orchestra. The Crown is more than a hundred years' old and is on the site of a medieval tavern that stood next to the London house of Oliver Cromwell, the Lord Protector of England during the nation's brief flirtation with republicanism.

The tavern is a former Taylor Walker outlet but has been transferred within the Allied Breweries group to the Nicholson's subsidiary, which runs its pubs as free houses, hence the good range of beers. The charming and comfortable pub has a small front bar divided from the rest of the interior by a few snob screens. The side bar has glazed windows, a carpeted floor, slim pillars and plenty of seating with half-panelled walls surmounted by flowered paper.

There is a tiny and intimate snug bar under spiral stairs leading to the first floor. The walls are crowded with prints of old London and playbills from the defunct Apollo Theatre which used to perform upstairs. A large and imposing clock in an alcove is connected with the 1683 Rye House conspiracy in Hertfordshire. This fascinating and intriguing information sent me hurrying to the small Georgian house a few doors away that houses the Marx Memorial Library and volumes of information about radical activity; but, alas, it shuts for the whole of August and I remain ignorant of the Rye House conspiracy. A second clock in the Crown hangs over the bar and purports to tell the time in Havana, Cuba, but is stuck fast at 12 noon; could this be an oblique political comment on Dr Castro's régime?

The bar serves rolls and sandwiches lunchtime and early evening. A large back room acts as a separate restaurant for lunches during the week. There are seats on the pavement, too. Clerkenwell also has a number of genuine Italian restaurants; the families of nineteenth-century Italian *emigrés* live and work in the area and hold occasional colourful carnivals and festivals. The excellent Clerkenwell Heritage Trust at 33–35 St. John's Square (tel 250 1039) has information on the area and organises guided walking tours.

≈ Farringdon

⊖ Farringdon

Places to see: St. James Church and Marx House

Eagle

159 Farringdon Road
Closed Sunday

✗ lunchtime

⊕ **Banks and Taylor Shefford Bitter, Eastcote Ale, SOS, SOD**

This spacious, one-bar pub, just a hundred yards up the slight hill from the Guardian's head office, is one of a clutch of London pubs leased by the enterprising small Bedfordshire brewers, whose SOS ale triumphed in the New Breweries section of CAMRA's 1988 Champion Beer of Britain Competition. The two married couples, the Desquesnes and the Ayres, who run the company, were not prepared to leave their tasty and distinctive ales to the vagaries – and slow payment – of the free trade and set out to build a bridgehead in the capital with their own tied trade outlets.

The Eagle, leased from Truman, has green as its colour theme (even though the colour is believed to be unlucky in the pub business) with ruffled green curtains and blinds at the large windows, hanging baskets that sprout ferns, lamps suspended from a green ceiling, plus bare board floors and plenty of seats. The walls are half-panelled and there is a real live piano against the wall: there are musical evenings several times a week.

The walls are crowded with a *pot-pourri* of old prints and pictures, a style that has become the eclectic theme of Banks and Taylor's pubs. Food is simple, filling pub fare: jumbo sausages, chicken and ham pie, burgers, ploughman's, salads and jacket potatoes.

The brewery logo is a cricket bat and it was

≈ Farringdon

⊖ Farringdon

---

fitting that, on one of my visits, I saw Alec Bedser, one of the greatest figures in post-war English cricket, supping a pint.

Finch's London Spa

70 Exmouth Market

✗ lunchtime

🍺 Draught Bass, Charrington IPA; Courage Best Bitter, Directors Bitter

It is hard to believe that this narrow street, with only a few desultory market stalls, was for centuries a leading spa and resort. A chalybeate spring, rich in iron salts, was discovered there in 1206 and quickly developed into a health and entertainment centre known as London Spa, which became renowned for the quality of the home-brewed ale in the tavern that rose with the spa. There are a few remains of the old spa in the cellar of the present pub, a vast and ornate Victorian gin palace which had a reputation at the time of being a house of "ill repute".

Finch's, with an imposing three-storey and dormered frontage across the road from Finsbury Town Hall, is now a free house but it was a Charington pub for many years as the occasional Toby Jug logos suggest. Charrington's parent company is commemorated by a splendid old "Bass & Co's" mirror at the far end of the saloon bar. This is a genuine old-fashioned two-bar pub. The smaller public bar is dimly lit and comfortable with deep leather benches. The whole interior is wonderfully tiled, has some leaded windows and floors that are part carpeted and part bare.

It is an impressive reminder of the considerable architectural effort that went into creating "decent" drinking places that would keep the working class out of the sleazy holes that dispensed rot-gut gin in the nineteenth century.

An enormous oval bar, with small lamps built into a canopy, dispenses drink to both public and saloon. The over-loud juke box is the only glaring note. Hot lunchtime food includes curry and rice, plaice and chips, sausage and chips,

🚆 Farringdon

🚇 Farringdon

Places to see: Sadler's Wells Theatre

steak and kidney pie, jacket potatoes and vegetarian quiche. Finch's was one of the first pubs to embrace the new flexible licensing laws and, when I visited it, was opening 11 am to 11 pm Monday to Saturday.

Fox and Anchor

115 Charterhouse Street
Closed weekends

✘ breakfast and lunch

🍺 **Ind Coope Burton Ale, Taylor Walker Best Bitter, Tetley Bitter**

The Fox and Anchor is the archetypal Smithfield pub, slap in the heart of the vast meat market where if, like me, you prefer not to eat flesh you will pass the butchery halls with averted eyes and try not to sniff the odours of meat. Because the market workers often labour during the night, some of the Smithfield pubs have special licences that allow them to open for breakfast. The Fox and Anchor opens from 6 am until 3 pm and serves hot food until 2.30 pm.

The narrow frontage is impressive with a fine example of *Art Nouveau* dating from 1896. It is now a grade II listed building. Inside, the pub is narrow and comfortable, with the bar running almost the full length of the building and tables and seats in a narrow passageway alongside. There are further dining tables at the rear of the pub.

The Fox and Anchor is a serious eating and drinking place and canny City workers have twigged that if it is where the Smithfield men eat then it must be both good and cheap. The impressively efficient staff serve up great plates of food ranging from egg and bacon breakfasts to vast mixed grills, chops and steaks at lunchtime. It is a jolly pub, with a lot of laughter and ribald humour of the market workers.

Even vegetarians should pay it a visit: take a deep breath and, like me, ask for egg and chips. The pub is just a short walk from St. John's Gate, one of the original and surviving entrances to the walled City of London.

🚇 Farringdon
🚇 Farringdon
Places to see: St. John's Gate

Old Mitre

Ely Court, off Ely Place and
Hatton Garden
Closed weekends

✕ lunchtime

🍴 seats in courtyard

🍺 **Friary Meux Bitter, Ind Coope
Burton Ale, Tetley Bitter**

The Old Mitre, tucked away in a tiny courtyard, is a few yards from the great jewellery centre of Hatton Garden: pause and look in the myriad shop windows at the glittering displays before searching for the old-fashioned street lamp that marks the entrance to Ely Court. The small two-bar tavern is a careful replica of an inn built in 1546 by Bishop Goodrich for the servants of his palace in Ely Place and has an air of great antiquity. The bishops of the great cathedral of Ely in Cambridgeshire used Ely Palace as their London base. For centuries the palace and the tavern were officially part of the Ely diocese and the inn was licensed by the Cambridge magistrates. City of London police are supposed only to enter the premises at the landlord's invitation, though the law is administered more in the breach than the observance. Shakespeare knew of Ely Palace: John of Gaunt's "This sceptr'd isle" speech in Richard II was made there.

The wood-built pub with its small windows has a larger back bar and tiny front one with beams, settles and oak-panelled walls. A busy central serving area dispenses pints, with snacks lunchtime and early evening.

The preserved trunk of a cherry tree inside the tavern marks the boundary of the land leased to Sir Christopher Hatton in 1576. Hatton not only gave his name to Hatton Garden but ousted the bishops, weakened their authority and took control of the area. Queen Elizabeth I, Good Queen Bess – a great ale quaffer – is rumoured to have danced around the cherry tree, no doubt after a quart or two. During the English Civil War the tavern was used both as a prison and a hospital, though its size suggests that it could have held only a handful of prisoners and war wounded.

When the Old Mitre is busy and the weather is clement, the cheerful throngs of drinkers spill out of the pub into the courtyard, where there

⊖ Chancery Lane

are a few bench seats. A few yards' away is St. Ethelreda's Church, the only London church that has reverted to Roman Catholicism since the Reformation.

Old Red Lion

418 St. John's Street
Closed Sunday

✘ lunchtime; evening snacks

🍴 seats in courtyard

🎭 upstairs theatre

🍺 **Draught Bass, Charrington IPA**

⊖ Angel

Places to see: Sadler's Wells Theatre; Business Design Centre

The Old Red Lion – known simply as the O.R.L. to its regulars – is just a few yards from the great road intersection called the Angel after another and now defunct tavern (it is now a Co-Op Bank). The pub, with its narrow, four-storey red brick frontage, topped by a handsome cornice, stands out from the smaller and drab buildings that surround it. Across the road is the modern, garish office block of British Telecom. The present pub was built at the turn of the century but there has been an inn on the spot for several centuries. The fine Victorian interior has been lovingly restored by the licensees, Tony and

*Old Red Lion
The Angel*

Pauline Sherriff-Geary, an East End couple with a lively and occasionally abrasive Cockney humour.

The large and plush interior has a most unusual design. The front area of the pub is a narrow passageway with a fine wood and engraved glass screen dividing it from the comfortable section set aside for lunchtime eaters.

The passageway, historically, is a right of way that links St. John Street with Goswell Road; the pub has a small second entrance in Goswell Road and a few tables in a tiny courtyard. The right of way means that pedestrians could, if they chose, demand to walk through the pub at any time but the response from the Sherriff-Gearys would be terse and in basic Anglo-Saxon.

Another legend is that the great Norfolk radical Tom Paine, who helped inspire both the American and the French revolutions, wrote the Rights of Man in the pub. The legend is inscribed in a text on the wall but, in fact, Paine wrote his tract in the American colonies. He was undoubtedly a regular visitor to the inn, for the area of Finsbury and Clerkenwell was for long a haunt of radicals (the next pub in St. John Street, the Crown and Woolpack, has a bust of V. I. Lenin in the bar: Russian revolutionaries held meetings in the upstairs room now used by the Ancient Order of Buffaloes).

The Old Red Lion is served by a long bar against the far wall. The food, cooked by Tony, who learnt the business in the Army Catering Corps, is excellent and is based on fresh ingredients supplied every day by local markets, butchers and fishmongers. There are always two or three hot dishes every lunchtime, including a vegetarian dish such as vegetable lasagne; the Friday fish dish, such as fisherman's pie or cod in a pastry envelope, should not be missed. The pub also serves one of the best-kept pints of Draught Bass in London.

The pub's other claim to fame is its tiny upstairs theatre (tel 833 3053 for details of performances.) There are regular plays, some of them experimental. A number of younger playwrights and actors have gone on to fame and fortune after appearing at the pub theatre. When the theatre is open there are often throngs of actorish people in the bar and occasional famous faces. According to the Sherriff-Gearys, one of the best-known names in the British theatre and cinema was once in the pub "as p****d as a rat".

Sekforde Arms

34 Sekforde Street
Opens 7.30 pm Saturday and Sunday evenings

✘ lunchtime; evening snacks only

🍴 seats on pavement

🍺 **Young Bitter, Special Bitter, Winter Warmer**

This cheerful little street-corner pub, with its long, low frontage and a few tables and chairs on the pavement, has a special place in my affections. In 1984, in a moment of professional stupidity, I agreed to write an article about the sewers of Islington and the men who cleaned and repaired them. The entrance to the sewers was via a manhole (or "personhole", as they say in these parts) in Sekforde Street opposite the pub. The stench was bad enough but when I saw my first rat I made my excuses, clambered back to the surface and spent several hours and pints recovering in Thomas Sekforde's arms.

I drank Adnams' bitter on that occasion, for it was then a free house. It has now been bought by Youngs and, I guarantee, will just go on improving. Although it is just a hundred yards or so from the elegance of Clerkenwell Square, this is a genuine, unspoilt boozer, used by local people as well as office workers.

It has half-panelled walls, a carpeted floor, an open fire and a dartboard in one corner. There is plenty of standing room in front of the bar, and tables and chairs round the walls and windows. A small back room with larger tables is used by diners, but both this room and an upstairs games room are earmarked for change by Youngs.

As the brewery is making a great effort throughout its tied estate to improve both facilities and food, watch out for tasteful changes in the pub. Not that there is anything wrong with the food served at present: a blackboard announces such delights as chicken Kiev, steak, mushroom and Guinness pie, chicken curry, plaice and chips, rainbow trout, vegetarian curry, vegetable curry and ploughman's.

The arms on the sign belong to Thomas Sekforde or Seckforde, a patron of Saxton the cartographer, a lawyer and Master of the Rolls, who retired to a house in the area.

🚇 Farringdon

🚉 Farringdon

EC2
City Pride

28 Farringdon Lane
Closed Sunday evening

✗ lunchtime and evening

⌘ **Fuller Chiswick Bitter, London Pride, ESB**

The City Pride is a runaway success for Fuller, Smith and Turner, the independent brewers from West London. The pub is often so busy that, whatever the weather, drinkers are forced to spill out on to the narrow pavement on the little street that runs from Farringdon Road to Clerkenwell Road, with a fine view of St. Paul's rising above Farringdon station. Fullers have devoted great energy and money to redesigning the small pub. The bar was formerly part of another Fuller's house, the Star and Garter at Kew Bridge, and the interior has been cleverly fashioned to give the atmosphere of an intimate private house.

As you enter, the bar is to the left, with just a few ledges and sills on which to perch glasses and plates. To the right, a couple of steps lead to a spacious back room with plenty of tables and chairs, and walls decorated with prints of London and some fascinating old tradesmen's signs. Stairs from the main bar lead to the Hogarth Room, which doubles as lunchtime restaurant and function room.

The discreet, small-windowed exterior includes a sign incorporating the cross of St. George and the sword of St. Paul – both part of the coat of arms of the City of London – supported by glaring griffins, the symbol of Fuller's brewery.

Excellent food from the servery facing the door includes lasagne, steak pie, sweet and sour chicken, chilli bean casserole and vegetable curry. Turn left when you leave the City Pride and you come to number eighteen Farringdon Lane, which houses the Clerk's Well that gave the area its name and also fresh spring water that encouraged not only brewers but such famous gin distillers as Booth and Gordon to set up in business. The well is at least one thousand years old.

≈ Farringdon

⊖ Farringdon

Places to see: Clerk's Well.

Dirty Dick's

204 Bishopgate
Closed Sunday evening

✗ lunchtime; separate
   restaurant and wine bar

🍺 **Charrington IPA; Courage
   Best Bitter; Greene King IPA,
   Abbot Ale; John Smith's
   Yorkshire Bitter; Webster's
   Yorkshire Bitter**

🚉 Liverpool Street

🚇 Liverpool Street

This ancient ale house, handily placed across the road from one of Liverpool Street station's many entrances, dates back to 1870 but the wine vaults are much older. It takes its name from one Nathaniel Bentley who lived near the pub in the late eighteenth and early nineteenth centuries. He was nicknamed Dirty Dick because of his reluctance to use soap and water. He was a City dandy who was so stricken with grief when his fiancée died on the eve of their wedding that he shut the dining room where the wedding breakfast was to have been held and left the contents to decay – a mournful event used by Dickens in "Great Expectations". He allowed the standards of cleanliness of both himself and his ironmonger's shop to decline to such an extent that customers crowded the shop on the assumption that there must be bargains among the dust and grime. When Bentley ran into

TRY HOBSONS WINE BAR UPSTAIRS

FINE WINES

Dirty Dicks, Bishopsgate

financial difficulties the shop was turned into a pub, complete with cobwebs and mummified cats.

The ground-floor bar has been cleared of all this detritus and is now a dimly-lit room with many side alcoves and stripped pine and bare timbers all round. The walls have been taken back to the original brickwork, the floors are bare and there are prints of old London and old wine casks acting as tables.

A barley twist staircase leads up to Hobson's wine bar and restaurant while a separate entrance takes you down to the vaulted cellar and an unfortunate din of piped pop. Bar food includes a daily hot special, plus ploughman's and jacket potatoes.

Olde Dr Butler's Head

Mason's Avenue, Coleman Street (off Moorgate)
Closes 9 pm; closed weekends

✘ lunchtime

🍺 **Courage Directors; Tolly Cobbold Original; guest beers**

🚆 Moorgate

⊖ Moorgate

Places to see: Barbican Arts Centre

Mason's Avenue is a step into the past. Belying its name, it is just a narrow alley of wonderfully restored half-timbered buildings, leaning slightly in from the perpendicular. The jewel of this remarkable early seventeenth-century byway is the inn built in 1616 by the redoubtable Dr William Butler, whose stern visage adorns the large sign that hangs outside the dark wood-panelled exterior. Although the "doctor" failed to qualify he nevertheless became the court physician to James I, an odd monarch who knighted a Loin of Beef and helped to arrange an honorary degree in medicine for Butler. The doctor brewed a famous medicinal ale in his tavern and also developed a "cure" for epilepsy that involved letting off a brace of pistols without warning a few feet from the hapless sufferers, who were probably cured of life as well as their affliction.

His inn today retains its low-beamed ceiling and bare board floors covered with sawdust. Just a few lamps light up the dim interior. Large mirrors advertise port and sherry and there are old wine casks, with prints and a large barometer on the half-panelled walls.

A servery at the raised back of the bar specialises in vast ploughman's lunches with a choice of cheeses, pâté, turkey and pork, plus chunky sandwiches. Full lunches are served in the first-floor restaurant with leaded windows and a Victorian chop house atmosphere. The bar staff downstairs dispense vast amounts of ale during the busy lunchtime period and offer such guest beers as Higson's deliciously hoppy bitter from Liverpool and a "house beer" – thought to be Courage Best Bitter – called Webster's, named after the company that owns the pub and which should on no account be confused with the Watney group's ubiquitous beer of the same name.

EC3
East India Arms

67 Fenchurch Street
Closed weekends

✕ lunchtime

🍺 **Young Bitter, Special Bitter, Winter Warmer**

This tiny and boisterous bar is a reminder that the River Thames is close by. The nature of commerce has changed but the area was once busily and prosperously engaged in sea-going exports, including beer. The great English ale that we now call bitter was originally known as India Pale Ale as a result of its popularity in the vast sub-continent: the ale was first developed in Burton on Trent for overseas trade but it became rapidly popular at home and began to overtake dark London Porter in popularity. Bitter is exported down many throats in the East India Arms, a cheery bar that older Londoners would affectionately call a "boozer". This is not a term of abuse but a signal to the world that a warm welcome is guaranteed to all in an atmosphere devoid of frills.

The one-room pub has a stone floor and dominating horseshoe bar with a plank frontage. To the right of the bar there is a fine mirror from the long-defunct Dartford Brewery in Kent, once a purveyor of "Fine Ales, Stout and Porter". The

≉ Fenchurch Street

⊖ Aldgate

pub is packed soon after morning opening, recalling the Victorian habit among City workers of "having a wet" to lubricate the day's efforts.

In common with all City pubs, the East India Arms closes early in the evening when the day's business is done and its customers pack a lot of eating and drinking into the comparatively short opening hours.

Food is good honest pub grub that will set you up for the afternoon: savoury rissole in a large bap, a king-size sausage similarly surrounded, cottage pie and lasagne should quell the most rumbling of tums. For those who prefer the grape to the grain there is a surprisingly good wine list offering Chateau Segonzac, Beaujolais Villages and Alsace Gewurtztraminer. When – and if – you leave this happy little pub spare a glance to the left to the brilliantly restored edifice of Fenchurch Street station.

Lamb Tavern

Leadenhall Market (off Leadenhall, Gracechurch and Fenchurch streets)
Closed Saturday evening and Sunday

✖ lunchtime; no smoking bar

🍺 **Young Bitter, Special Bitter, Winter Warmer**

⊖ Monument

Places to see: The Monument, which marks the site in Pudding Lane where the Great Fire of London started in 1666.

The Lamb is one of the City's finest old taverns, the centrepiece of a spacious and elegant covered market that once vied with Smithfield as the capital's main meat market. There is now a wider choice of goods on offer beneath the stately curved glass roof. From the top floor of the Lamb you can choose your comestibles from shops ranging from delicatessens to oyster mongers. The tavern and the accompanying buildings are painted a vibrant claret and cream, with heraldic griffins glaring and grimacing atop every pilar.

The Lamb, packed with market and office workers, was founded in 1780 by wine and spirit merchant W. Pardy but its present structure is a brilliant Victorian one, with masses of engraved glass and gleaming tiled walls, including a tiled painting in the entrance of Sir Christopher Wren outlining his plans for the Monument in 1671.

The vast ground floor bar is split-level, with a

wrought iron spiral staircase leading to a mezzanine area. The basement has both a wine bar and a smoking room with tiled walls and a curved bar; the twin dartboards are in constant demand.

A flight of stairs from the side entrance leads to the airy and elegant first floor lounge, decorated by portraits of Young's Brewery directors in Victorian times. The lounge is a smoke-free zone and the carvery has a great roast of beef and a choice of salads.

The Three Lords

The Minories (Tower Bridge end)
Closed weekends

✗ lunchtime; no smoking bar

🍺 **Young Bitter, Special Bitter, Winter Warmer**

Three or any number of lords would be a leaping after a session in this thoughtfully refashioned tavern. With plain board floors, snug side alcoves, banquettes and a cluster of hanging globes to give light, it has something of the atmosphere of a Whig coffee shop. The long bar runs almost the full length of one wall and allows plenty of standing room, which is a necessity as the pub tends to be busy even at times when decent folk are still waiting for the sun to reach the yardarm before downing the first pint of the day.

Wandering around City pubs brings home to you the fact that a lot of business is done early in the day in the area's many splendid watering holes; and I suspect that not a lot of work at all is done after lunch, if the prodigious amount of booze I saw despatched is typical of City gents' life style.

A servery at the end of the bar offers hot dishes at lunchtime, backed by an impressive and imaginative range of sandwiches, including prawn salad, tuna mayonnaise, beef in French bread, and egg mayonnaise.

The pub – which also has a basement bar where the noxious weed is banned – is named after three rebellious Jacobites, including Prince Charles Edward Stuart ("Bonnie Prince Charlie"), the last Stuart to attempt to regain the throne. If the many stories of his imbibing abilities are to be believed, he would have felt at home in this fine ale house where his and his relatives' histories are recounted in a series of illustrated wall panels. The street in which the Three Lords stands has an equally fascinating history. It is named after a minor order of nuns – a *minores* – who had a sanctuary in the area.

⊖ Tower Hill

Places to see: The Tower of London and Tower Bridge

EC4
Black Friar

174 Queen Victoria Street
**Closed Saturday evening
and all day Sunday**

✗ lunchtime and evening

🍽 seats on pavement

🍺 **Adnams Bitter; Boddingtons
Bitter; Draught Bass; Tetley
Bitter**

The wedge-shaped pub that lies back from the road at the junction of New Bridge Street and Queen Victoria Street is the most remarkable of all London's many architectural and historic ale house delights. It is *Art Nouveau* – not just the odd touch here and there but the full, florid brush strokes of that idiosyncratic *fin de siècle* style. The pub, built in 1903 from designs by H. Fuller Clarke and the sculptor Henry Poole, is a celebration of boozing, a temple for the bibulous. It pays homage to a great Dominican

priory of the order of the Black Friars, which stood on the site many centuries ago. The friars were more renowned for their dedication to the bottle than their devotions and their tippling is encapsulated in the great array of bronze and marble tableaux that decorate the pub inside and out.

At the narrow, arrow-head front of the building, above the street number picked out of the marble, stands the figure of a jolly, rotund friar, hands comfortably folded above his impressive beer belly. Panels running the length of the exterior show more friars urgently beckoning to passers-by to hurry in and enjoy the pleasures on offer.

Inside there is a profusion of red, green and white marble, with a mass of intricate bronze work. The finest section is the back room, reached through two archways. Great mirrors on the rear wall reflect the stunning marble and bronze, with a frieze of panels showing jocular friars fishing, singing and sleeping off their carousing. Not-too-serious engraved slogans advise customers that "Silence is Golden", "Wisdom is Rare" and "Industry is All". The main bar area has an enormous inglenook fireplace and a small horseshoe bar. The tiny front room, built into the tip of the wedge, serves a good range of imaginative food: hot lunches include lamb casserole, chicken marengo, jacket potatoes, and Cheddar, Brie, pâté and Stilton ploughmans; there is a cold buffet in the evening.

As a result of the enormous crowds that throng the pub, it had become a trifle faded. Nicholson Inns, the owners, deserve much praise for investing close on a million pounds in lovingly restoring the Black Friar to its great and rumbustious glory, a singular drinking house to which you, like me, will return again and again with undiminished pleasure. Nicholsons even removed the fruit machines, Bacchus be praised!

Be advised to visit the pub, if possible, before or after the lunchtime crowds. If it is too packed, you can stand or sit on the terrace in New Bridge Street. The Black Friar is a good base if you are visiting the Mermaid Theatre in Puddle Dock (founded by Sir Bernard Miles) or British Telecom's Technology Showcase in Queen Victoria Street, a fascinating illustrated history of the telephone and telecommunications.

≋ Blackfriars

⊖ Blackfriars

Places to see: Mermaid Theatre; BT Technology Showcase

Olde Watling

29 Watling Street
Closed weekends

✗ lunchtime

🍺 **Draught Bass,
Charrington IPA**

Watling Street is rich with the presence of Sir Christopher Wren. Both the inn and the great church of St. Mary-le-Bow next door were destroyed in the Great Fire of London in 1666. Wren redesigned them both and the pub was used by the workers building the church; St. Mary-le-Bow, according to legend, determines who are the true London Cockneys, for only those born within the sound of its bells can claim the name. (Cockney is a corruption of cock's egg, a thing of no use, the derogatory term used by country people to describe the stunted urban people of William Blake's Great Wen.) The Olde Watling is achingly old and two restorations this century have carefully retained its character.

It is built on a framework of old ship's timbers and the small ground-floor bar has beams and bare boards and is lit by many old lamps. The profusion of paintings includes thirty-one prints of Wren's City churches. Bar food includes spicy chicken, steak pie, and lasagne and salad. There is a hot and cold buffet in the tiny Wren Bar on the first floor.

From Watling Street, named after the great Roman road north from London, you can catch a glorious sight of St. Paul's Cathedral and imagine Wren standing on the spot watching his greatest creation slowly climbing skywards. Cricket buffs should note that another pub a few

⊖ Bank

Places to see: St. Paul's Cathedral, St. Mary-le-Bow, Mansion House, the Bank of England, the Stock Exchange doors away, called fittingly the Pavilion End, shows television coverage of important matches.

FLEET STREET
Olde Bell

95 Fleet Street
Closed Sunday lunchtime

✗ lunchtime

🍴 seats in churchyard

🍺 **Boddingtons Bitter; Marston Pedigree; Tetley Bitter**

A great deal of money and love from Nicholson's Inns has gone into restoring one of London's most historic drinking places. The small frontage with leaded windows carries the lettered title "Ye Olde Bell Tavern Wines and Spirits". The dimly-lit, low-ceilinged interior has stone-flagged floors at the front and bare boards at the rear. Clearly there were once two bars (at least) in this small, intimate but roomy inn, served by a central bar, with plenty of standing space and seating.

The Bell was built in "Fletestrete" in 1670 for builders working on St. Bride's Church, which had been badly damaged in the Great Fire of 1666. The name was an ecclesiastical obeisance to the church; earlier inns on the site had been named the Swan, Golden Bell and Twelve Bells. It has long had an association with printing, for the suitably-named Wynkyn de Worde, who followed in the thumbprints of the great English printer Caxton, sold books on the premises.

There is a rear entrance to the inn in a tiny alleyway reached from St. Bride's Lane. When the bar is packed and the weather kind, drinkers can stand in the alley or, better still, take food and drink and sit in St. Bride's churchyard.

The Bell offers a daily lunchtime hot special such as braised steak and two vegetables plus a full range of snacks. It stands just a few yards from the modern and functional edifice of the great news agencies of Reuters and the Press Association. Reuters began in the last century, using pigeons to carry the news of wars, famines and disasters; today both Reuters and PA use the most modern technologies to send the news to all corners of the world at the speed of light.

🚇 Blackfriars

🚋 Blackfriars

Olde Cheshire Cheese

Wine Office Court, 145 Fleet Street
Closed weekends

✘ lunchtime and evening; separate restaurant

🍺 **Samuel Smith Old Brewery Bitter, Museum Ale**

The modern world so stiff and pale/You leave behind you when you please/for long clay pipes and great old ale/And beefsteaks in the Cheshire Cheese wrote the poet John Davidson, commemorating one of the capital's greatest and most famous taverns. You can easily miss it as you find your way through the bustle of Fleet Street: watch for the sign inviting you into the suitably bibulous Wine Office Court where a curious, circular sign announces the presence of the sash-windowed inn. Ye Olde Cheshire Cheese reeks of history in its warren of small rooms, arranged higgeldy-piggedly over the three storeys of a smoke-blackened building with sawdust on the floors and blazing fires and ranges.

The site is ancient. The stone-vaulted stone-roofed cellar has a blocked passageway that once led to the Thames when the building was used by the brethren of the White Friars. A shaft with clear water in the cellar was once a monastic well. Above the cellar, the site made the easy transition from monastic one to ale house, was burnt down in the Great Fire and rebuilt a year later. It is now a listed and protected building.

Over the centuries it has had a grand and roistering reputation, used by the likes of Dr. Johnson, his faithful scribe Boswell, the painter Reynolds and that ubiquitous toper, Charles Dickens, who mentioned the inn in "A Tale of Two Cities". They would not notice many changes in the present pub, with its narrow, winding wooden staircases, crowded corridors, beer served through hatches and a Chop Room that serves its famous array of steak and kidney pie, game pie, roast beef and nursery puddings. Upstairs there is a second bar and another dining room; downstairs an oak-beamed cellar bar with an ancient, worn flagstoned floor.

⊖ Blackfriars

Punch Tavern

99 Fleet Street
Closed Sunday lunchtime

✗ lunchtime

🍺 **Adnams Bitter; Boddingtons Bitter; Marston Pedigree; Tetley Bitter**

Fleet Street today may be just a tattered and shrivelled reminder of its former gaudy and raucous self as the great centre of the national newspaper industry but it has retained its splendid old ale houses. And there are still many printers and journos left in "The Street": the Black Lubianka offices of the Express group are opposite the Punch while the Mail group is a quick stagger away in Carmelite Street, though both groups will eventually join the new-tech throngs in Wapping, the Isle of Dogs and Battersea.

The Punch has its own small piece of Fleet Street fame: it is named after – or gave its name to – the famous satirical magazine which was launched by a band of young radical journalists in 1841. They were keen to mock the less-than-appealing mores of the upper classes and the Monarchy (the present-day forelock-tugging attitude of the press to the Royals was not shared by the nineteenth-century prints).

The Punch, once a rather scruffy Victorian tavern, has been lovingly and painstakingly restored by Nicholson's Inns. The main entrance in Fleet Street is a long tiled and mirrored lobby leading into the large and ornate bar with a copper top, lots of vast mirrors on the walls and behind the bar, and many cartoons from Punch.

The great circular bar dominates the tavern, creating narrow passageways to the left and rear and several intimate areas. There is plenty of plush seating and a former separate public bar by the side entrance in St. Bride's Lane is now set aside for eating such lunchtime food as spicy meat balls, beef stew, lasagne, chicken curry and steak sandwiches. The Punch is often extremely busy and crowded but service is fast and efficient. Gentlemen drinkers should take care when visiting the "gents", which has an

🚇 Blackfriars

🚊 Blackfriars

Places to see: St. Bride's Church

awesome plunge to the basement and is the only known reason for drinking low-alcohol beer.

EAST LONDON

E1
Lord Rodney's Head

285 Whitechapel High Street

✖ lunchtime

☺ live music

🍺 **Banks and Taylor Shefford Bitter, Best Bitter, SOD**

The old East End good-natured cheer has not entirely disappeared. When I entered the bar, locals sitting near the door greeted me with a "Wotcher, mate" and bid me "cheerio" when I left. You don't get that in Chelsea. The Lord Rodney is one of the pubs in the small chain run by the enterprising Bedfordshire Banks and Taylor brewery. It is named after Admiral Lord Rodney, an eighteenth century buccaneer who defeated the French in the West Indies in 1782.

There is a noisy street market outside the pub which you enter by a large and airy front section with many tables and chairs. The long bar counter has a narrow passageway by its side and another large area at the back with more seats and a bar billiards table. The walls are crowded with the typical Banks and Taylor "job lot" prints and pictures bought from old shops: there is a rag-bag of Victorian and Edwardian country scenes, school photographs and seascapes. Green lamps and fans are suspended from the dark plank ceiling.

Good value lunches for around £2 a plate include cottage pie, steak and kidney pie, chilli, vegetarian goulash and ploughman's. Live music is staged at weekends. The pub, a most welcoming and attractive old East London boozer, is next door to the station and opposite the imposing façade of The London Hospital, the great teaching hospital involved in the attempts to cure the unfortunate Elephant Man. A lesser-known claim to fame is that my mother had a kidney removed there.

⊖ Whitechapel

Places to see: The London Hospital

Prospect of Whitby

57 Wapping Wall

✘ lunchtime and evening; separate restaurant

🍺 beer garden

🎵 live music

🍺 **Webster's Yorkshire Bitter, Ruddle's County**

⊖ Wapping

The Prospect pleases. This creakingly ancient riverside alehouse was built in 1520 and is named after one of the great sailing ships which plied between the North of England and the Thames. The area of Wapping is changing out of all recognition. It was once a riverside industrial region packed with warehouses and tenement blocks for the local people. But now Wapping is a New Tech area with matchbox offices and printing plants, plus ludicrously expensive apartments and "tine hises" for the new rich in the City of London. Such change may be inevitable in the brash, hard-faced era of the unbridled market economy but it is causing considerable hardship and resentment among the older residents.

Fortunately this remarkable tavern is unspoilt and unchanged, apart from the influx of younger people with raucous voices that clash with the East End dialect. The ceilings are low and beamed, the floor is stone-flagged, furniture is made from old beer and wine casks and there are wonderful views of the river from the vast bowed windows.

The pub has a grisly history. The infamous Judge Jeffreys, the "Hanging Judge", would hold trials in the area, watch the bodies of his victims hang in chains by the river and then retire to the Prospect to feast himself.

A great solid wood bar runs from just inside the entrance, the length of the main bar and then loops round to end in a food servery. There is an enormous open fire, a genuine pianola and ancient wooden pillar propping up the ceiling. At the back of the bar a tiny terrace overhangs the river where you can sit and sup. Opposite the servery, a large seating area with benches and wooden tables also overlooks the river. If you go out through the side door you are in a pleasant and surprisingly rustic beer garden, replete with weeping willow.

Simple and no-nonsense pub grub includes sausage, beans and chips, Cornish pasty and chips, vegetarian pasty, salads, ploughman's and filled rolls. The Pepys' Dining Room on the first floor offers full sit-down lunches and even finer views of the Thames. A singing guitarist performs every weekday evening and there is an Irish folk group at weekends. The Underground station is on the short East London section of the Metropolitan Line, which you catch by changing at Whitechapel and following the signs.

E2
Marksman
254 Hackney Road

✖ lunchtime snacks

🍺 **Bateman XB; Pitfield Bitter, Dark Star; guest beers**

A small wood-panelled one bar pub with a not too obtrusive military theme, it has been a flag-bearer for real ale in an area where many pubs are just lager-swilling shops and has graced the Good Beer Guide for many years. The Marksman has given great encouragement to the local Pitfield Brewery, selling its beer for some time now.

There is a rifle suspended from the ceiling and many old military artefacts on the walls and framed war-time newspaper cuttings. There is the ubiquitous East End pool table at the rear of the bar, behind a spiral staircase that ascends, rather surprisingly, from the centre of the pub up to the staff quarters. An abundance of comfortable seating is provided with stools, chairs and wall banquettes; the bar is light and airy thanks to large windows and a glass cupola in the ceiling. It is a busy pub and as well as a good passing trade has support from locals – taxi drivers, hospital workers, people in the motor trade and the occasional East End heavy – who ruminatively sup the local ale.

There were just basic lunchtime snacks when I last visited the Marksman but the licensee changed just as the guide was going to press and better fare may now be on offer.

🚉 Cambridge Heath

Ship and Blue Ball
Bundry Street

✖ lunchtime

🍺 **Pitfield Bitter, Hoxton Heavy, Dark Star**

This pub has several claims to fame. The Great Train Robbery was planned in the pub in the sixties: in the upstairs games room there is a false wall behind which the villains who robbed a British Rail mail train of several million pounds stashed some of their loot. Much earlier, in the late nineteenth century, one of Jack the Ripper's victims was found on the pavement outside the pub.

Its current fame is more pleasant: it is the first pub to be owned by the tiny Pitfield Brewery in Hoxton. The owners, two young Londoners

🚉 Liverpool Street
Ⓔ Liverpool Street

known affectionately in the trade as "the Yeasty Boys", started a specialist beer shop in Pitfield Street near Old Street. They spread their wings by brewing their own beer in the back yard and then moved to bigger premises round the corner in Hoxton Square. Their brews are splendidly tasty and fruity and in 1987 Dark Star, a strong ale like an old London Porter, won the prize of Champion Beer of Britain at CAMRA's Great British Beer Festival, a remarkable feat as Pitfield were competing against long-standing commercial brewers from all over Britain.

The pub is tiny and it is hard to believe that it was once a three-bar tavern. The bar top is tiled and there are seats around the walls. The licensee is the jovial Julian Farrow, a former London organiser of the Campaign for Real Ale, and he has plans to change and considerably improve this former Watney house, built in the early nineteenth century. He will decorate the

walls with brewery artefacts. Lunchtime food includes traditional bangers and mash, rolls and sandwiches.

Bundry Street marks the boundary of the two East London boroughs of Hackney and Tower Hamlets. The pub is on the Tower Hamlets side, which pleases Rob Jones and Martin Kemp, for Hackney Council had once offered Pitfield the lease of a pub near the brewery and then withdrew the offer. They are happier to be in Tower Hamlets. Opposite the pub is a block of flats that was built as an example of "model housing" for the working class in Victorian London and which replaced some appalling old tenement slums.

E5
Anchor and Hope

15 High Hill Ferry, off Harrington Hill

🍺 **Fuller London Pride, ESB**

If you are peckish, eat elsewhere for the Anchor and Hope doen't have time to bother with food. This tiny nutshell of a pub is one of the smallest in London and its draws crowds like a magnet from the surrounding estates as there are not many Fuller's houses in this part of the world. The landlord is kept busy pulling pints to please the punters.

The tiny bar faces you as you enter and to right and left are small areas to stand or sit; a dartboard is squeezed into one corner. On winter evenings when the pub is relatively quiet you can sink into a comfortable armchair and think you are deep in the countryside, and not just a hundred yards or so from the roar of the Lea Bridge Road.

When the sun shines customers create more room inside the pub by moving out on to the towpath alongside the River Lea, a commercial river whose banks are busy with warehouses and timber yards. To get to the pub you can either make your way down Harrington Hill from Upper Clapton Road or you can have a bracer in the Prince of Wales (see next entry) then cross

🚇 Clapton (closed Sunday)

Places to see: River Lea

the Lea Bridge Road and make your way along the tow path and through a timber yard until you come to the Anchor and Hope.

The name is not a nautical one: St Paul called hope "the anchor of the soul" and there are many variations on this religious theme, including Hope and Anchor and the Anchor in Hope.

Prince of Wales

146 Lea Bridge Road

✕ lunchtime

🍴 seats on terrace

🍺 **Young Bitter, Special, Winter Warmer**

The Prince of Wales is a great, old-fashioned East London boozer. Rather like an East End domestic house, it has a functional public bar for people in working clothes, where they can munch a sandwich with their beer and play darts, and an enormous plush lounge with opulent furnishings and posh wallpaper where customers put on their best clothes for a good night out.

The pub overlooks and in parts overhangs the River Lea. Windows in the lounge give a view of the river and in spring and summer you can sit on a terrace area with plenty of wooden seating to enjoy your beer and watch the river and energetic oarsmen go by.

At weekends the old and fast-disappearing East London tradition of eating seafood is kept alive at the Prince of Wales. A covered stall offers such delicacies as shrimps, prawns, winkles, mussels and whelks. There are also good, satisfying pub lunches during the week.

I used the Prince of Wales for several years when the cricket team I played for had its home pitch next door on Millfields recreation ground. The plan of action each Sunday was tried and tested: we would meet at the pub, have a couple of pints, then stroll round to the ground to flash the willow. The only problem was that if the game finished early (it usually did if I were batting) it meant that, due to the silly Sunday licensing laws, we had to kick our heels and wait for the pub to open again at seven o'clock.

� Clapton (closed Sunday)

Places to see: River Lea

E6
Boleyn Tavern

1 Barking Road, corner of Green Street

✗ snacks lunchtime and evening

🎵 live music

🍺 **Ind Coope Burton Ale, Taylor Walker Best Bitter**

They don't build pubs like this any more. It is a wonderful example of Victorian rococo, an enormous pub built at the time when brewers had profits pouring out of their pockets and created vast drinking palaces for the working class. The Boleyn must at one time have been a hotel or boarding house as it stands three-storeys high and dominates this busy road junction. The great windows are etched and inside there are more etched screens and high moulded ceilings.

Those who complain about the decline of the two-bar pub have nothing to moan about here, for there are no less than three. The front bar is narrow; through a door and sharp right and you come into the great main bar with seats running along the far wall and room at the back for a pool table. Keep going and you come to yet another small bar, probably once a snug or a jug-and bottle* bar, that faces on to the Barking Road.

The carpets are a bit tatty and the tavern is in need of a lick of paint but it stands as a fine example of a late nineteenth-century ale house. I have known it for more years than I care to recall for I passed it on my way to school, to West Ham football ground next door and, finally, to my place of work. It offers live music on Thursday, Friday and Sunday evenings. During the week there is a pleasing mix of customers but it is best to avoid it when West Ham are playing, as the bars tend to fill up with young men with bovver boots, shaven heads and Union Jack tattoos.

Although it is difficult to believe, the pub takes its name from Anne Boleyn, one of the hapless wives of King Henry VIII; her house stood close to the present football ground.

⊖ Upton Park

Places to see: West Ham United FC

---

*a jug and bottle was an early off-licence where customers brought their own jugs to be filled.

E8
Lady Diana

95 Forest Road

✗ lunchtime and evening

🍺 **Fuller London Pride; Pitfield Bitter, Dark Star; Young Bitter, Special; guest beers**

The name is a recent one and breaks the unwritten code that pubs are not named after members of the Royal Family until they are dead. There is a picture of the Royal personage on a wall, showing how she was before the Buck House image makers got to work on her. That aside, this is a most welcoming, beautifully-appointed, spick and span pub with flock wallpaper and comfortable upholstered benches and chairs. The small bar has a mirrored and

wood backing and gilt lettering offering "fine wines and brandies" and the walls are decorated with fascinating old prints of the area.

It is a genuine locals' pub, with people coming from the surrounding council flats and houses. It is also indisputably an ale house; not much lager is drunk and it is good to see older people tucking into pints of Pitfield beer.

As well as the excellent ale, the "Lady Di", as the pub is inevitably known, offers a rare treat – genuine pizzas. The landlady is a jolly Italian and has no truck with frozen apologies for the real thing. The pizza bases are made from proper dough and you then choose from a range of toppings: beef, salami, pastrami, mushroom and peppers. The pizzas are enormous and wonderful value for money. The simple menu also offers ploughman's and salads. Another welcoming

London Fields (closed weekends), Hackney Central, Hackney Downs touch is the air-conditioning system that keeps the atmosphere pure and free of nicotine fumes, the better for you to enjoy your pint and your pizza.

Taylor's

Martello Street

✘ lunchtime and evening

🍺 beer garden

🎭 live music

🍺 **Boddingtons Bitter; Fuller London Pride, ESB; Marston Pedigree**

🚊 London Fields (closed weekends), Hackney Downs

Graham Taylor has brilliantly transformed a drab and empty old Truman pub into a lively and spacious free house with a delightful view over London Fields, a large park that runs right up to the pub walls. Reaching the pub is not the most pleasant walk: you come under a railway arch, past a scrap metal yard and some gypsy caravans guarded by ferocious dogs (don't worry: they're chained) and then suddenly you're alongside the park and there is the pub announced by a large inn sign.

Inside there is a strong whiff of the David Bruce Firkin style (see entry for Falcon and Firkin, E9): bare boards, lots of pot plants in some unusual and fetching holders, brewery and advertising artefacts and, a survival from the

Scenes from the Lady Diana

past, an enormous old Truman mirror. There are plenty of tables and benches plus a few seats on a small raised area at the front of the pub, which is used for live music at weekends and some weekday evenings.

To the right of the bar is a food servery, with dishes chalked on a blackboard behind it. The food is imaginative and well-prepared. There is always one vegetarian dish each day such as mushroom or courgette bake or lasagne or vegetable curry, plus hot meat dishes, salads and ploughman's.

You can eat and sup in the pub or on pleasant days go out to a small walled beer garden overlooking London Fields. If that is crowded, do not despair, for a flight of stairs takes you down

to a second beer garden surrounded by high walls and with plenty of seating. It makes a good family area. Other customers tend to drift with their drinks on London Fields where football and cricket are played: Taylor's has its own cricket team.

The pub is busy and popular, particularly with staff from nearby Hackney town hall: they belong to the trade union NALGO, which wags say stands for "Not A Lot Going On". I have only one quibble about Taylor's, which has raised pub standards in the area, and that is that beer prices are high.

If I get some money off Roy today - cash ...

E9
Falcon and Firkin

274 Victoria Park Road

✗ lunchtime and evening

🍺 beer garden

⊕

🍺 Falcon Ale, Hackney Bitter, Dogbolter; guest beers

This is one of the chain of pubs built up by a remarkable young entrepreneur called David Bruce. He started his first Firkin (old Dutch for a nine-gallon beer cask) when he was on the dole and sold the lot in 1988 for six and a half million pounds to Midsummer Leisure, who promised not to make any fundamental changes. The Bruce style was a wonderfully simple yet immensely successful one. He developed fun pubs for all the family. All the Firkins – now much copied by envious bigger brewers – have bare boards, lots of terrible puns on T-shirts, brewery memorabilia on the walls, a pub piano, excellent and cheap pub grub and beer brewed on the spot.

The pub-brewery theme recalls the time before the rise of the big commercial brewers when almost all publicans brewed their own ale. In most of the Firkins it is possible to watch the brewing process through portholes in the wall or the floor and it is this aspect that gives the pubs their greatest attraction.

The end products are not especially remark-able beers and as they are kept under carbon dioxide pressure they do not qualify as "real ale". But they are pleasantly drinkable (though Dogbolter is alarmingly strong) and each Firkin always has at least one guest beer on handpump, such as Marston Pedigree or Shepherd Neame Master Brew for the *aficionados*.

David Bruce not only opened fun pubs but placed many of them in areas that commercial brewers would shun. The Falcon is a case in point. If you wanted to make money from a pub you might not choose Hackney as your port of call. But the pub is packed and popular and draws families from a wide catchment area. It is based in a surprisingly verdant part of Hackney, next to the great stretches of Victoria Park. In summer customers can use the large beer garden at the rear of the pub.

🚃 Cambridge Heath

Places to see: Victoria Park

The Falcon is a large pub. To the right as you enter there is a sizeable area given over to long tables and benches. To the right of the bar a food servery offers fine fare at remarkable prices – nothing over £2 when I was last there but inflation may have forced slight increases. Daily specials include chicken and bacon flan with salad, beef tatties and peas, or cheese and onion pie. The centrepiece of the food in all the Firkins is the giant baps – you choose your filling from various meats and cheeses. There is a more restricted menu in the evening.

To the left of the long bar there is a large family room known as Bo Junglies with a mass of fun things for children to play with and on. Throughout the pub there are paintings, prints and stuffed versions of falcons. It is a splendidly cheerful and unfussy tavern that proves that you can make pubs available to people of all ages if you put your heart into the venture and don't consider women and children to be nuisances.

E14
Five Bells and Bladebone

Three Colt Street

✗ lunchtime

⊲ **Ind Coope Burton Ale, Taylor Walker Best Bitter**

This is a true old dockland pub, close to Blackwall Tunnel, which links East and South East London under the Thames, and the great but now largely defunct West India Docks, once a major dock when London was the hub of the British Empire. The pub is surrounded by streets with such intriguing names as Shoulder of Mutton, Ropemakers Fields and Barleycorn Way, all indicating their links with the docks and imports. The pub was first called just the Five Bells: when ships in the docks rang five bells (2.30 pm) drinkers knew it was time to leave the pub, for 2.30 was then the traditional end of the lunchtime session in the East End. The "bladebone" was added when several razor-sharp knives were found on the site of an old abbatoir that supplied London markets with meat. Both the bell and the bladebone hang above the bar.

⇝ Stepney East

The dockland theme is underscored by the rear wall of the pub, which is made of old hessian sacking and ships chandlers' artefacts. A ship's wheel is built into a partition as you enter the pub. An illuminated display panel has a Toby jug of Lord Nelson and ships bric-à-brac. The walls are oak panelled and the bar illuminated by hanging lamps.

I felt immediately at home in the front section of the pub, which is like an old East End parlour – the "best room" used only for Christmas, weddings and funerals. It has deep and comfortable armchairs, a carpeted floor (the rest of the pub has bare boards), prints on the walls and the hallmark of the respectable working class – net curtains at the windows.

Lunchtime food in the pub includes plaice and chips, burgers, scampi, salads, sausage and chips, and steak and onion pie. Opposite is the

"Debbie" – in the
Five Bells and Bladebone
August 1988

splendid but sadly neglected structure of Lime-house Parish Church.

It was in the Five Bells and Bladebone that illustrator Phil Evans and I had what I shall delicately call something of an adventure. While I was making notes, Phil spoke to an attractive young woman sitting alone. After a few minutes he started sketching her. I joined them and we chatted about how the area had changed and how most of the pubs in the East End were now lousy. By this time the landlord had called "time" on several occasions and finally told us to leave. As the three of us made for the exit, the landlord pulled Phil and me to one side and whispered urgently: "I hope you realise that that 'woman' is actually a man!" In the best journalistic tradition, we made our excuses and left...hurriedly.

Grapes

76 Narrow Street

✗ lunchtime and evening; separate restaurant (not Monday evening or weekends)

🍺 **Friary Meux Best Bitter, Ind Coope Burton Ale, Taylor Walker Best Bitter**

The street in Limehouse is indeed narrow and is crowded on the river side with old warehouses. But many of these have been converted into studios and apartments for the well-heeled new arrivals in the area. Dr David "When I was Foreign Secretary" Owen, leader of the Social Democratic Party, lives next door to the pub when he is in London. The Grapes – a grade II listed building – is likely to outlast his splinter party. The pub was built at the end of the fifteenth century and was immortalised by Dickens, who called it the Six Jolly Fellowship Porters in "Our Mutual Friend."

The tiny frontage with a frosted glass motif in the windows leads into a small half-panelled bar with cream-painted walls packed with paintings of old boxers and bare-knuckle prize fighters. A large and fine oil painting by Alice M. West, called Saturday Night in the Grapes, was exhibited at the Royal Academy in 1949 and now hangs in the bar. There is a short bar

🚃 Stepney East
🚇 Stepney Green

counter. In front of it there is a small seating area with green covered benches. The floors are bare boards and a pair of scales hangs from the ceiling.

Additional seating is found beyond the bar and then a couple of steps lead up to a small terrace with large windows overlooking the Thames. A lady sitting in the window solemnly informed me that she often saw cormorants diving for fish in the river and seals basking in the water, but she may have partaken too much of the excellent and dangerously potable Burton Ale.

The food is something special. Not being a sectarian, I have detailed all the fleshy beast foods on offer in pubs in London but it gives me great personal pleasure to say that the Grapes is a fish-only pub and restaurant. Food includes plaice and monk fish plus rolls and sandwiches. My cod in crab sauce was delicious, the best lunch I had whilst compiling this guide.

When the pub closes, time is rung on an old ship's bell. You are unlikely to befall the fate of drink-sodden customers in the nineteenth century who, as Dickens wrote, were rowed out to the middle of the Thames, drowned and their corpses sold to anatomists for dissection ... though it is rather unnerving that the man who lives next door to the Grapes is known in political circles as "Doctor Death".

NORTH LONDON

N1
Albion

10 Thornhill Road

✘ lunchtime and evening;
restaurant section

🍴 terrace and beer garden

🍺 **Ruddles County, Webster's
Yorkshire Bitter**

The Albion is an elegant old tavern in a winding street of fine houses and mews cottages at the heart of the genteel and gentrified area of Islington. The origins are probably Georgian; it was once a coaching inn as the arch to the side of the pub testifies. The frontage is low-slung and ivy-covered, with hanging baskets and old coaching lamps. There are seats and a few tables on a terrace, which is fenced off from the road. Through the door and you are into a large main room with a vast, solid and highly polished old bar counter to the left and a cheerful, airy section to the right with dining tables that is used as a lunchtime restaurant and is warmed by a blazing open fire in winter. In the bar area the walls are wood panelled and have seats built below the small windows.

A passageway between the bar and the dining area has smaller rooms leading off where you can enjoy a quiet drink in wood-panelled charm. If you keep going down the passage you come to an enormous beer garden with trellis work and climbing roses and other flowers and plants. A barbecue area is used at weekends in the summer months.

The beer garden is extremely popular in fine weather and is an ideal spot for parents to take young children. The pub has a vast range of food, from proper sit-down three course lunches with soup, roast and something-with-custard for pudding, to quiche, ploughman's and filled jacket potatoes.

The bar counter tantalisingly has a range of small, truncheon-like pump handles that serve nothing at all but which must have once delivered a good range of ales when Watney was a London regional brewery. Now it is part of a great international conglomerate, Grand Metropolitan, which thinks in global terms and offers just two heavily-hyped traditional beers from separate and newer pumps. *Chacun à son goût,*

🚇 Caledonian Road

🚇 Angel

but I find the ubiquitous Webster's a thin, bland beer brewed neither to offend nor excite the tastebuds, while the strong and fruity Ruddles County is not a lunchtime drink, unless you plan a post-prandial slumber.

Albion is a name of Celtic and subsequently Latin origin for England; it acquired a derogatory connotation at the height of England's sea power when the country was known by its enemies as Perfidious (treacherous) Albion. Many fighting ships of the Royal Navy were named Albion.

Compton Arms

4 Compton Avenue, off Canonbury Lane

✖ lunchtime

🍺 outside drinking area

🍺 **Greene King IPA, Abbot Ale, Rayment BBA**

🚃 Highbury and Islington

⊖ Highbury and Islington

In the dog days of real ale in the early seventies, when London was officially designated a "beer desert" by CAMRA, the Compton kept the flag flying with an excellent range of cask beers. It was bought by Greene King a few years ago, which has restricted the choice of beer, but it remains a splendid little alehouse with a unique character. When I worked in the area for several years it was always a pleasure to turn in to Compton Avenue – a cobbled mews in spite of its grand title – from the traffic's roar in Canonbury Lane and Upper Street and approach the tiny, one-storey cottage pub.

The small windows of the pub are just a couple of feet clear of the pavement. You enter through a small door with low head clearance into the narrow bar area. The floors are bare boards and the ceilings are low. To the right there are a few tables and chairs, some of them down a couple of steps. To the left the bar swings right and takes you into a separate room with wooden benches and chairs and a dartboard.

The main bar has many charming old prints of the ancient London borough of "Isledon" – the modern Islington. A door at the side leads to a tiny terrace with crazy paving and tables made from old beer casks under a sycamore tree. Hot lunches are excellent value and highly imaginative; I enjoyed a memorable seafood pancake with salad; carnivores can get their teeth in to chilli con carne, jumbo sausage in French bread and chicken Maryland, with ploughman's, salads and filled jacket potatoes.

The pub is popular with staff from nearby Islington town hall. It is worth having a look at the building, one of the most impressive pieces of municipal architecture in London and in great demand by film and TV producers to shoot such disparate productions as Minder, Superman II and a crime series based on Raymond Chandler's short stories. The town hall was built in the early 1920s and, to the embarrassment of the current left-wing council, has the "fasces" symbol carved below the roof that was used by Mussolini's fascists in Italy.

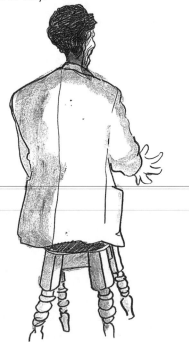

Crown

*Corner of Cloudesley Square and
Cloudesley Street*

✗ lunchtime and evening;
separate dining area

🍺 outside drinking area

☺ children welcome

🎵 live music

🍺 **Fuller Chiswick Bitter, London
Pride, ESB**

The Crown is a superb Edwardian pub, bought by Fullers from Ind Coope and lovingly restored; it richly deserved a prestigious award for the best pub refurbishment from CAMRA's Pub Preservation Group in the mid-eighties. The green and gold marble effect wallpaper, above wood panelling, looks rather like Sage Derby cheese. There are glazed glass partitions, potted plants in handsome *art nouveau* containers, some on plinths, draped windows and a great solid oval wood bar decked out with original snob screens and lamps. An old stove, which gives out welcome warmth in the winter, is surmounted by an old "Fuller, Smith and Turner" mirror. The walls are decorated with prints of Edwardian London and leather benches provide comfortable seats.

To the right of the fireplace, an alcove leads into the eating area, where parents can take children. This area, with some fine mirrors on the wall, used to be in the same style as the rest of the pub but Fullers, mistakenly I feel, have modernised it and it now looks like a cross between a Paris *brasserie* and a post-war ABC cafeteria.

The food is high quality, with hot dishes of the day – beef cooked in ESB, shepherd's pie, chilli, plaice and chips, steaks – plus excellent ploughman's with a choice of Stilton, Cheddar, Camembert or Brie, toasted sandwiches and ploughman's.

There are two entrances to the pub, one in the square and one in Cloudesley Street, a wide avenue with some attractive turn-of-the-century houses. In front of this entrance there is a small paved area fenced off from the street and laid out with benches and chairs, a delightful place to eat and drink in good weather. This very superior pub offers live music at the weekend.

↔ Angel

Places to see: Business Design Centre (the former Royal Agricultural Hall) in Liverpool Road

Eagle Tavern

Shepherdess Walk, off City Road
Closed Saturday

✖ lunchtime and midweek
   evenings; Sunday roast lunch

🍺 **Draught Bass, Charrington
   IPA**

The Eagle is such a famous London pub that it has a Cockney song – which has achieved international status – dedicated to it: "Up and down the City Road/In and out of the Eagle/ That's the way the money goes/Pop goes the weasel". As you may recall from the entry for the Castle in Cowcross Street, EC1, "popping" is the Cockney expression used when exchanging a family heirloom for money in a pawnbroker's shop. In the late nineteenth and early twentieth century, workers in the Old Street area clothing industry who were – pardon the pun – hard pressed for cash, would pop their "weasel", a type of flat iron, for the wherewithal to sink a pot or two in the tavern.

It is a most impressive building, its elegant green-painted exterior topped by a dome and surmounted by a gold eagle. At the same time as the clothing workers and tailors were popping their weasels, the Eagle was part of a large complex that included the Grecian Theatre, a vast music hall where such stars as Marie Lloyd sprang to fame and acclaim.

The Grecian has long since disappeared but the Eagle maintains its sturdy vigil in the area. The main bar is enormous, with plenty of seats, brown decor and mock gas lamps hanging from the ceiling. The walls are crowded with old prints of the Grecian Theatre period. The great central bar also serves a delightful small side bar with wood-panelled walls, more seats and a fine Bass Pale Ale mirror.

Imaginative food from a large servery in the main bar includes a hot daily special such as lamb stew, plus ploughman's, salads, scampi, salmon and plaice and chips.

The name of the pub is yet another religious and heraldic one; it has been used as an inn sign since the fifteenth century and decorated church lecterns as the symbol of St John the Evangelist. Even earlier, the eagle was the insignia

⊖ Old Street

of the Roman legions who invaded many parts of Europe and the British Isles and survives today as national emblems in many countries, including Germany and the United States.

Hen and Chickens

Corner of St Paul's Road and Canonbury Road (Highbury Corner roundabout)

✗ lunchtime snacks

🎭 theatre upstairs

🍺 **Young Bitter; Draught Bass, Charrington IPA**

This fine old Charrington house on the corner of one of the great traffic snarl-ups in North London is like a time machine in reverse; by some optical illusion it manages to be smaller inside than out. From the road you seem to be approaching a substantial tavern, with a Hen and Chickens motif picked out in a cornice on the top floor. Inside, however, it is a comfortable, snug and cosy one-room pub with a great slab of solid oak for the bar, bare-boarded floors, and walls that are part wood-panelled and part tiled.

The walls are decorated with old theatre bills and there is some fine glazed and engraved glass in the interior doors and in some unusual wall panels. The outstanding feature of the pub is the splendid old Charrington Toby jug mirror in a wooden frame that hangs above the fireplace. You go up a flight of stairs by the bar to a small live theatre, the Corner Theatre. (Islington is remarkable for the number of pubs with theatres; we have already come across the Old Red Lion in St John Street and there is also the King's Head, best known of them all, in Upper Street, and the Hemingford Arms in Hemingford Road.)

Food in the Hen and Chickens is confined to sandwiches, but these are enormous "doorsteps" with cheese, ham and corned beef which should keep the average stomach quiet for an hour or two.

The pub name has a fascinating history. According to Leslie Dunkling and Gordon Wright in their excellent "Dictionary of Pub Names" (Routledge and Kegan Paul), one deri-

🚉 Highbury and Islington

⊖ Highbury and Islington

Places to see: Highbury Fields

vation is the seventeenth-century nickname for Pleiades, the group of stars in the constellation of Taurus, a second is a late nineteenth-century name for a compound daisy such as the London Pride and, most likely of all for a pub sign, the London slang terms hen (large pewter pot) and chickens (smaller pewter pots). There are only glass pots in the present pub but you can fill them not only with the house beers but also with Young's Bitter; Bass and other big brewers are sensibly offering the Wandsworth ale to discerning drinkers in a few chosen outlets.

Cross the road from the pub and then turn right and you come to Highbury Fields, a large open expanse of parkland, one of the nicest public parks in North London.

The pub bore

Marquess Tavern

32 Canonbury Street

- ✕ lunchtime and evening
- seats on pavement
- **Young Bitter, Special Bitter, Winter Warmer**

- ⇌ Essex Road
- ⊖ Highbury and Islington

This palatial boozer, built in the 1950s, stands alongside the delightful New River Walk, a tree-shaded park and stream that was once a vital supply of fresh water for North London from rural Hertfordshire. The small doors at the top end of the pub open on to a fine front area with a large horseshoe bar surmounted by a gantry for glasses. To the right a small section that used to be a separate public bar is set aside for darts players and older locals who like a quiet pint. To the left is a larger area with a handsome fireplace and real live fire.

The back room through a curtained alcove is the high point of the pub, with a high ceiling, a

The pub comic

calm and elegant atmosphere, heavy embossed wallpaper, marble pillars, chandeliers and lamps built into seat rests. Lost for words amongst all this ornate splendour, I asked my friend Lynne for help with a description. "It's like a Turkish brothel," she said, quick as a flash. I have to bow to her superior knowledge of these matters but I doubt if there are many houses of ill repute in Istanbul that serve Young's Bitter and have a portrait of the Queen Mother on the wall.

To cap it all, the Marquess serves some of the tastiest pub food in London. Marquess Red Pie is corned beef and potatoes in a crust, and you can also have plaice and chips, an excellent vegetable curry with popadoms and mango chutney, stuffed pancakes, pasties, curry pasties, and ploughman's. Lovely grub and reasonable prices.

It is worth strolling around the area, for it is a slice of Islington at its most fascinating, with the sprawling Marquess council housing estate, drab municipal offices and elegant, ivy-covered town houses in Canonbury Square.

Waterside Inn

82 York Way (corner of New Wharf)

✗ lunchtime and evening; separate restaurant

🍴 drinking terrace

🍺 **Adnams Bitter; Boddingtons Bitter; Brakspear Bitter; Greene King Abbot Ale**

🚃 King's Cross

⊖ King's Cross

The Waterside works, even though it is a cunning fake. A warehouse on the Regent's Canal has been turned into a pastiche of an old London oaky beamy inn. Usually I would run a mile from such an absurdity but the Waterside gets away with it because it has been done well. You have to search for it, because it lies well back from York Way, the thoroughfare that leads up from King's Cross. From the outside it is a cleaned up brick warehouse with a large inn sign showing a boat on a canal. Inside there are wooden beams and pillars, bare board floors and a great open fire that appears to be live until you notice after a while that the coals never change shape nor turn into ashes.

As you enter through a narrow door at the

side of the building you are confronted by the long bar running half the length of the spacious room. Beyond it, the room opens out into a larger seating area, with sheltered alcoves to the right and a raised and enclosed area to the left.

At the far end of the room, large wooden doors take you out on to a terrace overlooking the canal. Moored alongside is a canal boat, the Floating Lady, that is owned by the pub and has been turned into a restaurant. When the weather permits it is a delight to sit on the long terrace, sip a pint of ale, watch the canal and wave to the citizens of Islington; the stretch of water marks the boundary between the boroughs of Camden and Islington. In winter, the fire may be fake but it belts out a most welcoming heat. There is a nice touch in the side alcoves in the form of little switches in the ceiling which you can use to turn off the canned music – but the tapes are better than average and often feature Duke Ellington.

At right angles to the bar is a large food servery that offers ploughman's, vegetarian dishes, quiches and salads. The food may have improved since my last visit before the guide went to press, for the pub had just been bought by Whitbread though, curiously, it was then selling no Whitbread beers. The pub has had a short and chequered history; it was a free house under a strong Bass influence, then it was bought by the tiny Hoskin's Brewery in Leicester. As such it drew drinkers like a magnet, anxious to partake of the remarkably fine ales from the East Midlands. Then suddenly it changed hands again and Whitbread were in control.

Much miffed by the loss of the only Hoskin's outlet in London, I tackled managing director Barrie Hoar: "I sold it," he said, "because I can buy three or four pubs in the Midlands from the money I made." The loss is a tangible one. The

Waterside remains an engaging watering place but the range of beers is commonplace for London and if I have made you fancy a pint of Hoskin's bitter you will have to go to Leicester.

N6
Flask

77 Highgate West Hill

✗ lunchtime (snacks Sunday); separate restaurant

🍺 outside drinking area

🍺 **Ind Coope Burton Ale, Taylor Walker Best Bitter, Tetley Bitter**

⊖ Highgate/Archway

Places to see: Karl Marx burial place and bust in Highgate Cemetery, Kenwood House and grounds

The Flask is an enormously popular North London ale house, rich in history and fine furnishings and decorations. It should not be confused with its Hampstead namesake, though the origins of the title are identical (see Flask, NW3). This building is ancient, first erected in 1663, rebuilt in 1767 and, save for an extension, mercifully left alone since then. It lies back from the road and is fronted by a large courtyard with cherry trees, benches, tables and some old wooden highbacked settles. The frontage of the inn is most attractive, with a wood-pillared portico, small leaded windows, hanging baskets and an inn sign showing a cheerfully bucolic scene of trees, sheep and a shepherd's crook.

Inside the pub is a warren of old wood-panelled rooms with copper jugs hanging from the beams, more high backed settles and service through a sash window; you have to stoop to order your drinks. Steps lead up to the more spacious modern room, which has a tiled floor, settees and Windsor chairs, and is used mainly for people who are eating.

Food includes shepherd's pie, vegetarian pie, roast beef, jumbo sausages, filled jacket potatoes, ploughmans, salads, quiche and sandwiches.

The Flask has been used by a number of famous — and infamous — people down the centuries. The highwayman Dick Turpin escaped from his pursuers at the inn (he is also said to have had an escape tunnel from the Wrestlers, another Highgate pub), and William Hogarth, George Cruickshank and Karl Marx were regulars. Hogarth lived on the site of yet another famous North London pub, the Old Bull and Bush in Hampstead; on one outrageous occasion, friends of Hogarth's attacked a customer in the Flask with a tankard and the artist in turn was attacked when he attempted to sketch the proceedings. Marx, in spite of his serious political intentions, was a jovial toper, given to long pub crawls with his collaborator Engels. Marx is buried close by in Highgate Cemetery.

The Flask, in common with other Highgate pubs, is famous for the ceremony of the Swearing on the Horns, which involves kissing a pair of antlers tied to a pole. Those who take part are granted the freedom of Highgate if they swear to drink strong ale, "nor kiss the maid when the mistress is about but sooner than miss a chance, kiss them both".

Highgate village has many fine houses and shops. If you go by car it is also worth visiting Kenwood House in Hampstead Lane. This fine stately home is owned by the Iveagh Trust and is open to the public. It has magnificent rooms and fine paintings, including some original Constables. Concerts are often staged in summer in the grounds.

N7
Flounder and Firkin

54 Holloway Road

✗ lunchtime and evening

🍺 **Fish T'Ale, Whale Ale, Dogbolter; guest beers**

🚊 Highbury and Islington

⊖ Highbury and Islington

This is one of the best-kept and most entertaining of the Firkin range (see Falcon and Firkin, E8 for background). The beers brewed in the cellar have some of the worst puns of all David Bruce's brews; you can see the mini brewery through glass-covered observation holes in the floor at the rear of the pub.

It was transformed from a derelict Ind Coope pub in the mid eighties and the low-slung frontage is decked out with welcoming lamps. Through the doors and you are confronted with the usual Firkin atmosphere of no nonsense bare floors, functional bench tables, a mass of brewery, pub and fishy memorabilia on the walls, an open fire and T-shirts for sale with more awful Bruce puns.

The raised area at the back is slightly smarter and quieter, except when the live piano is belting out old favourites. The pub is enormously popular and does a lot of noble work for charity by organising fun runs.

The food is nourishing and good value, with daily hot dishes and the famous Firkin baps with choice of fillings. The house beer is not "real ale" by CAMRA's strict definition but there is always at least one guest Real McCoy available on handpump.

NW1
Prince George of Cumberland

195 Albany Street

✘ lunchtime

◪ **Bateman XB; Greene King Abbot Ale; Whitbread Flowers Original; guest beers**

A welcoming and comfortable pub – but not recommended for members of the Stuart clan or supporters of the Jacobite cause, for it is named in honour (sic) of Duke William Augustus, the younger son of the Hanoverian George II. The duke defeated Charles Edward Stuart – Bonnie Prince Charlie – at Culloden in 1746 and then put down the remaining Jacobites with such terrible savagery that he was nicknamed Butcher Cumberland.

It's a nice wee drinking shop for a' that, with half wood-panelled walls, green carpets, a green-painted ceiling with globe lights suspended from it and brown upholstered wall seats. There is some fine engraved glass in the doors, and large and splendid mirrors behind the solid polished wood bar that has unusual wooden pillars on it topped by circular glass holders and light globes.

The Prince George is a rarity, a genuine free trade pub, not one owned by a big brewer that masquerades as a free house by selling beers from other companies whose shares are controlled by Big Brother. Try the Bateman's bitter, a lovely quenching, nutty ale from a small brewery in the Lincolnshire Fens.

⊖ Regent's Park/Great Portland Street

Places to see: Nash Terraces, Regent's Park

The food is somewhat rudimentary and, as you would expect in a house dedicated to Duke William Augustus, there is a strong emphasis on flesh; pork chop and chips and beef burgers. What, no Cumberland sausage?

The military theme is carried on in Albany Street, which has an army barracks. To the left of the pub are the stunning Nash Terraces, some of the finest Regency architecture in London, and beyond lies Regent's Park, with the golden onion dome of the London Mosque rising above the trees.

Spread Eagle

141 Albert Street (corner of Parkway)

✖ lunchtime

🍴 seats on pavement

🍺 **Young Bitter, Special Bitter, Winter Warmer**

⊖ Camden Town/Regent's Park

Places to see: Regent's Park, London Zoo

This is one of the most welcoming of all Young's many splendid London pubs. It was my first visit in several years when I dropped in to give it the once-over for this guide but I felt at home straight away. It was also clear that the brewery has carried out a little bit of remedial work – new wallpaper here, new curtains there – but done with that touch of concern and care for the feel of a place that the bigger brewers rarely match.

As you walk up cosmopolitan Parkway, with Asian restaurants and Italian delis, the pub immediately appeals to you, with its cheery seats and parasols on tables on the pavement and a pub sign depicting an eagle spreading its wings – a sign whose origins go back to Roman times and which also has been used for centuries by some noble English families. The bar that faces Albert Street has wood-panelled walls, carpets, old prints and photos of the area, heavy brass lamps suspended from the ceiling and green upholstered walls, stools and tables.

A narrow passage leads into a larger bar that overlooks Parkway, with curtained windows and plenty of comfortable seating. A smaller wood-panelled room leads off from this bar and is used for serving food at lunchtime. Imaginative lunches include poacher's pie, lasagne, cauliflower au gratin, ploughman's and sandwiches.

One of the most pleasant aspects of the Spread Eagle is that it enjoys genuine local support and is not just full with transient customers. If you go early in the morning or evening, you will find a good mix of Camden Towners who engage in cheerful banter and swap gossip – some good natured, some vitriolic (the most interesting) – about their neighbours.

Be warned of the steep and perilous descent to the basement gents. In the unlikely event that you sup too deep of Young's ale, you can get a nasty feeling of vertigo as you stand at the top of the stairs that lead down to the place of easement.

The pub is a good watering hole if you are on your way to the verdant pastures of Regent's Park and the London Zoo.

NW3
Flask Tavern

14 Flask Walk

✗   lunchtime

🍺   beer garden

🍺   Young Bitter, Special Bitter, Winter Warmer

The boisterous Flask is one of Young's most popular pubs, so popular that at weekends the bars cannot cope with the crush and drinkers pack both the small beer garden at the rear and the pavement of the mews at the front. It is a large old boozer, a throwback to the days when Hampstead was not so absurdly expensive that the working class could not afford to live there. The pub reflects the old mix of people, with a plain public bar and a rather grand if slightly down-at-heel saloon, like a Duchess who has seen better times but who does her best to keep up appearances.

The inn sign on the solid three-storey building shows a soldier in nineteenth-century uniform drinking from a flask on the field of battle. In common with the Flask in Highgate (see entry), the name recalls the time when the tavern would provide flasks for customers to get fresh drinking water from the springs on Hampstead

⊖   Hampstead

Heath and Parliament Hill, though it is likely that the soldier on the sign was consuming something stronger than water.

There is a splendid cross-section of folk in the spacious, carpetless public bar, with pensioners quietly supping their pints in the corner seats as they have done for decades while younger and more fashionable people discuss such vital matters as the quality of the ale and the latest cricket scores. You can actually see both flat caps and cravats in the public bar of the Flask, and Camden Council should waste no time in placing a preservation order on it.

A deep and solid oak bar serves the public and runs into the saloon, which has carpet on the floor, mirrors and pictures on the walls, and deeply comfortable chairs and sofas. To the left doors lead in to the beer garden, which has benches and seats, is overhung by the branches of a tree and is a most pleasant place to sit and sup when the weather allows. The bar supplies basic pub grub, such as ham, egg and chips and sandwiches but food is not the first priority for people using the Flask.

Hampstead is still a popular place of domicile for actors and writers and you can often spot a famous profile or two in the Flask. It is frequented by members of the London Symphony Orchestra who enjoy a pint or two before a performance; I once asked one of them how they could play after supping deep of Young's beer. "From memory, dear boy, from memory," he replied, passing his glass to the bar for a refill.

My good friend Michael Hardman, a founder member of CAMRA, recalls the rather unnerving experience of watching the film Ten Rillington Place on television and the following night standing next to John Hurt, who played the hapless Timothy Evans, in the outside gents' toilet. "You were hanged last night," Hardman told him. "That's right," Hurt cheerfully agreed, adjusted his dress and returned to the bar. The Flask is that kind of pub.

Holly Bush

Holly Mount, off Heath Street

✖ lunchtime and evening (not Sunday or Monday evenings)

◉ children allowed in eating area

♨ live music

🍺 **Benskins Bitter, Ind Coope Burton Ale, Tetley Bitter**

⊖ Hampstead

Places to see: Hampstead village, the heath and ponds

A faint, illusory mist seems to hang about the lamp-lit exterior of this lovely and atmospheric pub, which offers a trip back to Victorian and Edwardian London when Hampstead was a genuine village on the fringe of the city – the home of the bourgeoisie with an enclave of writers and artists. The tavern was a favourite drinking place for Dr Johnson, the ever-present James Boswell, and Charles Lamb.

To find the Holly Bush from the station, walk up the steep rise of Heath Street; as soon as you pass another pub, the Nag's Head, on the left get ready for the short but sharp clamber up the steps to Holly Mount. The small pub, decked out with hanging baskets and illuminated by a Victorian street lamp at night, is on a bend to the right when you pause for breath at the top of the steps. The rambling warren of a building dates back to well before the time of Queen Victoria. It was once the home of the painter George Romney, who died in 1802; what were once his stables now form the back bar. On his death the building was sold to Hampstead Constitutional Club, who in turn sold it to a local licensed victualler.

He was made an offer he could not refuse by the Watford-based brewery, Benskins, who acquired a rare London outlet for their beers. In the fullness of time and according to the strict and ineluctable laws of the market economy, Benskins were submerged into the mighty conglomerate of Allied Breweries, the Watford brewery was pulled down and production of the beer was moved to Burton on Trent.

The front bar and rooms have a fund of Benskin's artefacts on the panelled walls. The front section is still lit by gas lamps that are more than seventy years old. There are old high backed settles, a dark and sagging ceiling and glazed partitions. To the right is a large and plainer section dominated by the large curved bar. A narrow passage leads into the George Romney room, less successfully refurbished with ochre-painted brickwork, though there is a fine Ind Coope mirror (reflecting another arm of the great Allied octopus).

A servery between the two rooms offers such tasty home-cooked dishes as beef in Burton pie, pork in cider, chicken casserole and chilli con carne.

The joy of this unspoilt old pub is that, even at its busiest, there are always quiet corners where you can enjoy your ale and conversation in an atmosphere that recalls a time when the village was 'Appy 'Ampstead and artisans rubbed shoulders with rising entrepreneurs, artists and writers.

The name of the tavern is dedicated to the bush that has marked a drinking place since Roman and Saxon times. While the bush now conjures thoughts of Christmas and Santa Claus, its original use was more bibulous. It was used by the Romans during the riotous events of Saturnalia, while the Saxons would hang a bunch of evergreens outside an alehouse to show that fresh beer had been brewed. Even today brewers with a sense of history display a bush outside a new pub on its first day of business.

NW8
Crockers

24 Aberdeen Place

✗ lunchtime and evening

🍺 seats on pavement

☺ in music room

🎭 live music

🍺 Arkell Kingsdown Ale;
Boddingtons Bitter; Brakspear
Bitter; Crockers Best Bitter;
Darley Thorne Best Bitter;
Greene King Abbot Ale;
Theakston Old Peculier;
Ward Sheffield Best Bitter;
Vaux Samson

⊖ Warwick Avenue/St John's
Wood

Places to see: Lord's Cricket
Ground

Take a deep breath – you are entering London's most amazing pub. Forget the street outside, for you could be sailing on a Cunard liner in the 1930s, with great state rooms, moulded ceilings and revolving ceiling fans. "Sumptuous" is the first description that springs to a clichéd mind, but it does not do justice to this remarkable building. It has a sad yet funny history, built at the height of the great Victorian railway boom by a speculative builder named Frank Crocker.

Mr Crocker was advised – no doubt by the Victorian equivalent of Arthur Daley – that Marylebone Station was due to be built on the precise spot where he was keen to build a hotel. With customers and a fortune waiting in the wings, Crocker spared no effort or money in rushing up an ornate building called the Crown, with bars and restaurants on the ground floor and guest rooms reached by sweeping marble staircases. When it was finished, Crocker stood back to admire his handiwork only to have the information imparted in his delicate shell-like that the station was going to be moved a mile down the road.

Alas, poor Crocker, a man with ideas above his station. He was bankrupt and, in despair, flung himself to his death from the roof of his finest if empty creation. Londoners, with their renowned morbid sense of humour, nicknamed the station hotel (sans station) "Crocker's Folly". The name became better known than the original and when the pub was bought in 1983 by the Vaux Brewery of Sunderland they renamed it simply Crockers.

The main bar area is a riot of marble – marble pillars, marble bar counter, marble fireplace (pity about the fake gas fire) and even marble walls. The ceiling is an astonishing piece of intricate purple and gold relief moulding and the windows have engraved glass. The Music Room through an archway is spacious and elegant, rather as I expect a gentleman's club to be, with ceiling fans, another marble fireplace, hanging baskets, plush sofas and chairs and even a stag's head on the wall.

The public bar on the other side of the pub looks almost plain by comparison but must rank as one of the best-appointed bars for working chaps in the capital, with green leaded windows, gilt cherubs and – a nice touch – a bar billiards table.

The bar staff are friendly and mainly comprised of Australians; perhaps they came over to see a Test Match between England and Australia at Lord's cricket ground round the corner, went to Crockers for a drink and decided to stay. Who can blame them? They bring a pleasant, down-to-earth attitude to the pub that gells remarkably well with the elegant surroundings.

Food from a large servery in the marble bar-cum-entrance hall includes braised kidneys, Somerset pork chops, smoked mackerel, ploughman's pie, vegetarian pie, salads and sandwiches. Live music is staged several nights each week and there are tables and chairs on the pavement if you find the interior decoration is too overpowering and you need fresh air.

Vaux, who also own Ward of Sheffield and Darley, have brought a fine range of ales to Crockers, including a house beer, several beers from other companies and a wheat beer, Wiezenbier, brewed at Sunderland; although they have given it a Germanic title, wheat beer used to be brewed widely in country districts in England.

The pub is understandably popular, no more so than when the crowds from Lord's come round during the lunch-break in a match or when rain stops play (about every ten minutes during the summer). Even if you hate or don't understand the English summer game, do go and look at one of the finest sporting stadiums in the world. But don't drink there – the beer is fizzy and wickedly expensive. Confine your drinking to Crockers and raise your glass in memory of the sad man who bequeathed it to St John's Wood and who is claimed to haunt the place, still waiting in vain for the trains to stop across the road.

Rossetti

23 Queens Grove

✘ lunchtime and evening, separate restaurant (closed Sunday)

🍴 seats on pavement and patio

🍺 **Fuller London Pride, ESB**

⊖ St John's Wood/Swiss Cottage

The London pub provides surprises round every corner. Who would expect to find a place of great elegance and dash designed in honour of Dante Gabriel Rossetti, the poet and painter and one of the luminaries of the mid-nineteenth-century Pre-Raphaelite movement? Fullers have lavished care and attention on one of their great showpiece pubs and have adhered to Rossetti's belief in strong primary colours in the furnishings and garish pink-painted statues of Roman and Greek heroes.

The floors are tiled in Roman fashion, the low ceilings are spot-lit, and wicker-work and pot plants abound. The pub is split-level, with the top floor given over to a restaurant which enjoys a deserved reputation for quality cuisine. The ground floor is sunk below road level. You enter past an outside patio area with tables, seats and a great gnarled tree, cross a small gallery and then go down a short flight of steps into the main bar. The counter has a mirrored front and the beer pumps are dwarfed by a large Gaggia espresso coffee machine. There are comfortable wall seats, and wicker-work chairs and tables. Pictures of Rossetti decorate the walls.

The bar is manned by a boisterous Italian with a handlebar moustache, who dispenses ale, coffee and food. The printed menu offers a range of salads, pâté, quiche, gala pie, turkey, Virginia ham, pizza Rossetti, lasagne and moussaka.

Purists may object that the Rossetti is not a

typical pub. The answer is that there is no such thing as a typical pub and this one, blazing with passion and *joie de vivre*, is a place to savour, enjoy and return to.

Swiss Cottage

Junction of Finchley Road and Avenue Road

✗ lunchtime and evening

🍺 **Samuel Smith Old Brewery Bitter, Museum Ale**

There is a London tradition of naming major road junctions after pubs, such as the Angel, the Boleyn and the Crooked Billet. Perhaps the best-known is the Swiss Cottage, a flamboyant building designed like an Alpine mountain building of Brobdignagian proportions and teetering on the edge of being kitsch. It has been pulled back from the edge by Sam Smiths, who paid a rumoured £1 million for the site and, with their usual devotion to style and tradition, have turned it from a tatty disaster into a place of surprising elegance and charm.

Beneath the sloping roof – rarely covered by snow – and the first-floor galleries and curlicues, are two main bars. The Victoria and Albert is beautifully appointed with wood-panelled walls, dark mottled wallpaper, stripped pine doors and bars, Victorian lamps suspended from the ceiling and deep leather armchairs and free-standing settees. The walls are decorated with old prints of the area.

A separate public bar has bare wooden floors, a dartboard and photographs of the Samuel Smith brewery in Tadcaster and the famous horses that pull the beer-laden drays. Sensibly, there is a separate games room so that people addicted to pool are kept away from serious drinkers, who are saved from having cues impaled up their nostrils.

Food includes home-made steak and kidney pie and chips, filled jacket potatoes, jumbo sausage and chips, ploughman's and sandwiches. There is a large patio area at the front of the pub with tables and benches where custo-

⊖ Swiss Cottage

Places to see: Hampstead Theatre Club

mers can enjoy food and drink and watch the famous Swiss Cottage traffic jam.

The pub is across the road from the Hampstead Theatre Club, which stages many fine productions that later find fortune in the West End.

Fatuous question No. 8763270

SOUTH LONDON

SE1
Anchor

Bankside

✗ lunchtime and evening;
separate restaurant

🍴 riverside terrace

☺ welcomed in restaurant and
garden

🍺 **Courage Best Bitter, Directors
Bitter**

An atmospheric old alehouse rebuilt in 1750 with a rich and colourful history. It is best approached from Southwark Bridge, making your way along the narrow and winding streets and mews alongside the river until you come to Clink Street: the pub is on the next corner. A notorious debtors' prison stood in Clink Street and older Londoners still refer to prison as "the clink". The Anchor is a maze of small, low-beamed and wood-panelled rooms, one of them named the Clink Room and menacingly replete with police truncheons.

The Anchor has a dormered roof, bowed windows and hanging baskets. Steps take you down into the bars, with their sunken floors, wooden pillars, prints of old London, dim lighting, small counters and food servery. There are high back settles and leatherette chairs to sit on. Narrow stairs take you up to a more spacious first-floor room called the Boswell Bar; another bar is named after his mentor, Dr Johnson, who vies with Charles Dickens for the astonishing number of London inns and taverns he drank in. The room with the food servery includes a glass cabinet with a model of Shakespeare's Globe Theatre, which stood nearby (on the way to the Founders Arms – see entry – you pass the site of the planned re-construction of the theatre).

Another flight of creaky stairs leads up to the Chart Restaurant, which seats one hundred and has some fine views of the Thames. Samuel Pepys is believed to have watched the spread of the Great Fire of London in 1666 from the Anchor and recorded "one entire arch of fire above a mile long, the churches, houses, and all on fire at once, a horrid noise the flames made, and the cracking of houses at their ruine".

Across the road from the inn is a large raised terrace area on the edge of the river. There are wooden tables and benches for customers and the terrace is popular and packed in spring and

🚃 London Bridge

⊖ London Bridge

Places to see: Clink Street, site of Globe Theatre

summer. To the right of the pub and through an arch is a large beer garden where barbecues are held in fine weather. Back in the pub, bar food includes steak and kidney pie, beef goulash, cauliflower cheese, game pie, quiche and salads.

Anchor Tap

28 Horsleydown Lane (south end of Tower Bridge)

✖ lunchtime and evening

◎ no smoking rooms

🍺 **Samuel Smith Old Brewery Bitter, Museum Ale**

The biter is bit! The Anchor was the first pub owned by John Courage when he bought the Anchor Brewery alongside Tower Bridge. In a modern morality tale, Courage got big ideas, bought the John Smith's brewery in Tadcaster, was in turn taken over by the fags, crisps and sauce group, Imperial Tobacco, which was then bought by the Hanson Trust who sold off the various parts to the highest bidders and Courage ended in the fizzy embrace of the Australian Elders IXL, which manufactures Foster's lager.

The Anchor Brewery has been closed and is now being turned into apartments for the sort of people who did well out of Big Bang and like to park their Porsches in full view of the neighbours. Meanwhile, the other Smith's brewery in Tadcaster, that of Samuel, retains a powerful commitment to traditional values and sturdy Yorkshire independence (if it has been bought by an Aussie lager maker by the time this guide appears, I will eat my beer mug). Sam Smiths now owns the Anchor Tap and a plaque on the wall records its history with a *soupçon* of glee and told-you-so.

The pub and the former brewery date back to the late eighteenth century. There are three tiny rooms up narrow stairs in this small, wood-panelled old alehouse. Two rooms have spectacular views of the great bridge and workmen transforming the old Courage building. There are two open fireplaces and plenty of comfortable seating in the form of banquettes, and captain's tables. The walls are decorated by a mass of

🚃 London Bridge

⊖ London Bridge

fascinating old prints of the area. The two front bars are served by a central counter and food servery offering steak and mushroom pie, pasta Bolognaise, cheese and onion quiche, sausage, beans and chips, ploughman's and salads.

The ground floor section of the pub was not open when I visited the Anchor but the management say it will soon be in full operation and will provide family facilities.

When John Courage opened his brewery at Horsleydown in the 1790s, it was an area of elegant houses, famed for the quality of the local entertainment in Southwark. The official Courage history suggests that the brewery was named Anchor as a result of its waterside connections and the considerable trade carried out by barges and ships. But John Courage was of French Huguenot stock and may have recalled St Paul's remark that hope was the anchor of the soul. Tap is short for taproom, a simple alehouse where casks were tapped or vented in view of the customers. A pub that is part of a brewery grounds or next to it is known as the brewery tap and traditionally is the first outlet to serve fresh casks of beer.

Founders Arms

52 Hopton Street, Bankside, off Southwark Street

✗ lunchtime and evening; separate restaurant

🍴 riverside terrace

🍺 **Young Bitter, Special Bitter, Winter Warmer**

🚆 Blackfriars

🚇 Blackfriars

A former pub of the same name marked the spot where foundries forged the bells for Wren's new St Paul's Cathedral, rebuilt after London's devastating Great Fire. Wren lived nearby and would watch his great masterpiece rising on the other side of the river. As the cover photograph shows, there are few grander and more inspiring sights than to sit in the present-day pub and watch the sun go down and the spotlights pick out St Paul's and the wedding cake spire of St Bride's, which in turn reflect their shadows in the Thames.

When Youngs were asked to build a new Founders Arms in the late 1970s to provide succour for a housing complex they avoided the temptation to build some awful fake-and-flummery "old world" tourist haunt. (There is such a place in St Katherine's Dock – it should be under water – called the Dicken's Inn, with plastic beams, serving wenches, Merrie England meals and decidedly modern prices: discriminating users of this guide will not be seduced). Such a building would have jarred monstrously with the great muscular and phallic 1930s Bankside power station that looms over the area.

Youngs sensibly plumped for a functional modern design that offers superb views of the river from a long wall made entirely of glass. It is a brilliant concept of one room built at so many angles and with free-standing "elbow rest" pillars that it appears to be divided into several intimate areas. Seating is provided by semi-circular green plush banquettes, and there is a carpeted floor and heavy lamps suspended from the brown and gold mosaic ceiling. The bar runs

along the wall opposite the terrace windows and serves all the nooks, crannies and alcoves. At the far end of the pub and beyond a partition there is a separate restaurant. A large terrace has chairs and tables with parasols.

Bar food offers a hot daily special, Cumberland sausage, quiche, ploughman's and a wide range of salads.

To get to the Founders, either follow the road from the Anchor, Bankside or, if you are coming across Blackfriars Bridge from the north, take a flight of steps down to the river on the left-hand side of the road and follow the narrow path round until you reach the pub.

George

Off 77 Borough High Street

✖ lunchtime and evening; separate restaurant

🍺 **Boddingtons Bitter; Brakspear Bitter; Greene King Abbot Ale; Wethered Bitter; Bulmer Traditional Cider**

⇌ London Bridge

⊖ London Bridge

Places to see: Southwark Cathedral, the Hop Exchange (Borough Road), the Monument.

Yes, it *is* genuine. The George is so achingly old and creaking that cynics might feel it was put up in the 1970s when nostalgia swept Britain and we all went around humming Glenn Miller tunes and replaced gas fires with open coal-burning ones. But the George has stood on this spot since Elizabethan times and is the last galleried inn from that period still standing in London. It hides rather shyly down an alleyway off the A3 road and once provided accommodation as well as food and drink for travellers on the great coach route to Kent and the port of Dover. That same route also brought hops from Kent to the capital and the borough of Southwark became a major brewing centre, based around the Hop Exchange, a vast and ornate building now being restored to its former glory; it was here that brewers bought and bargained over the price of the little green climbing plant that gives bitterness to beer.

Courage, Barclay Perkins and Thrale all had breweries in Southwark and Dr Samuel Johnson, a regular visitor to the George before dining with the Thrales, was profitably involved in the sale of his friends' Anchor Brewery to Barclay Perkins, coining at the time one of his less harmonious phrases: "We are not here to sell a parcel of boilers and vats, but the potentiality of growing rich beyond the dreams of avarice".

Southwark was an area of entertainment as well as boozing. Shakespeare's Globe Theatre was close by (the site and plans for actor/director Sam Wanamaker's re-creation of the Globe can be seen on Bankside) and his strolling players performed in the courtyard and from the galleries of the George. Mr Wanamaker has revived that tradition and you may also catch Morris dancers and jugglers performing at the

The 'Parliamentary Clock'

inn. The original inn was destroyed in the Great Fire of London in 1666, which ravaged most of Southwark. The spot where the fire broke out in Pudding Lane is marked by the Monument on the other side of London Bridge.

The George was rebuilt in 1677 and once occupied three sides of the courtyard. But its owners, the trustees of Guy's Hospital, sold it to the London and North Eastern Railway Company in the nineteenth century and the Victorian railway barons, in an act of unforgiveable vandalism, tore down parts of the inn to make way for engine sheds. The sheds are long gone but the inn remains, its presence marked by a sign in Borough High Street.

The ground floor bars of the George are small and low-ceilinged, with lattice windows, bare-boarded floors and wooden settles. The back bar, the nearest to the main road, has an old Parliamentary Clock, recalling the time when parliament, in one of its mad moods, imposed a tax on timepieces. The serving area through a small low hatch has a fine example of a Victorian "cash register" beer engine, the small pump handles sliding up down grooves in a wooden frame. A narrow corridor leads to a long central bar and then into a more spacious and elegant area used for eating. Simple fare includes sausage, beans and chips, home-made steak, kidney and mushroom pie, ploughman's and sandwiches. A superb central staircase leads up to small dining rooms and a gas-lit balcony.

The large courtyard has trestle tables and bench seats and is thronged by drinkers at lunchtime and early summer evenings, revelling in this proud and historic inn, named in honour of St George of England. As long ago as 1598 the George was noted as one of London's "fair Inns for the receipt of travellers", a fitting tribute that needs no embellishment four hundred years later.

Hole in the Wall

Mepham Street

✗ lunchtime only

🍺 **Adnams Bitter; Arkell Best Bitter; Everard Tiger; Greene King IPA, Abbot Ale; King & Barnes Sussex Bitter; Young Bitter; Draught Bass; Ruddles County (range liable to change)**

A good place for a rumble – but not in the American sense! This small, crowded and long-standing real ale oasis is built into one of the arches of Waterloo Station. Put your pint down and the liquid heaves in the glass while the whole building shakes as a train judders overhead. The main bar at the back of the building has a dark painted vaulted ceiling that is part of the rail arch. A gas lamp and two giant tulip-shaped electric lights descend from the dimness above.

The range of beers is enormous and constantly changing, though you should find some of the beers listed here: Young's bitter is a regular feature. The bar groans under the weight of all the beer handles needed to serve the beers, and there is also Murphy's stout from Ireland and Hacker-Pschorr *bier* from Munich. There is plenty of standing room in front of the bar and there are stools, round tables and settees against the far wall. A food servery dispenses lamb curry, pizzas, burgers, sausages, beans and chips, and sandwiches.

In contrast, the tiny and comfortable front bar is quieter and more comfortable with a smaller range of beers on the counter; the bar has more of the atmosphere of a back-street Paris café than a pub.

The Hole in the Wall is owned by the redoubtable Irishman Ulick Patrick Burke: the bar is also known as Burke's Free House and he has several other such establishments in London. Long before London pubs took to cask beer with enthusiasm, Mr Burke provided an outlet in his mews bar for a number of regional brewers to try their wares on the capital's drinkers.

The pub is popular with commuters using the vast and ornate station named in honour of the Duke of Wellington's defeat of Bonaparte. It is also a useful place to go for a drink before tackling the maze of the South Bank with the National Film Theatre and the Royal Festival Hall: it is certainly cheaper to drink in Mr Burke's establishment than in the South Bank bars.

≉ Waterloo

⊖ Waterloo

Places to see: South Bank complex

Horniman's

Hay's Wharf, off Tooley Street and Battle Bridge Lane

✕ lunchtime and evening; morning coffee; afternoon tea; separate restaurant

🍴 patio

🍺 Adnams Bitter; Arkell Best Bitter; Boddingtons Bitter; Ind Coope Burton Ale, Tetley Bitter

Hay's Wharf was once a dockside area of great warehouses, a hub of London's sea-going trade. One of the companies that used the wharf was the tea-trading firm founded by the Horniman family. When the docks left London for new container ports further down river, Hay's Wharf was brilliantly transformed into a galleria of shops, restaurants and – fronting the river – a pub named Horniman's in honour of the tea traders. The central area of the galleria has a soaring vaulted glass roof, picture and photograph exhibitions on the tiled floor and a brilliant life-size interpretation in iron work of a galleon.

The pub, a Nicholson's Inn, is a controversial concept. Its designer's claim that "it will be to the 1980s what the Black Friar was to the 1900s" is open to debate. My first instincts were hostile and I wrote that it was "less a pub and more a recreation of a British colonial club in pre-war Malaya where I half expected to see Willie Maugham glowering in a corner as the Mem Sahibs chattered over their pink gins."

But the place does grow on you and the pub as a concept is not fixed in aspic but must evolve and change. You reach the pub from a patio overlooking the river and the daunting grey bulk of HMS Belfast, which is moored close to the shore and is reached by a gangway; to the right there is a good view of Tower Bridge. A narrow balcony just inside the doors has stairs leading down to a sunken bar area. A massive polished mahogany counter runs the length of the room and round a corner where it merges with a food servery. Pillars on the bar are topped by globe lights, and similar lights and revolving fans are suspended from the ceilings. The place drips with potted plants of all descriptions and the walls are decorated with African, Egyptian and Indian artefacts that commemorate the imperial tea trade.

A large room at the back of the ground floor

🚇 London Bridge

🚉 London Bridge

Places to see: Tower Bridge, Tower of London, HMS Belfast, London Dungeon has deep, comfortable chairs and sofas while a sweeping staircase leads up to the first-floor restaurant; Horniman's has taken all-day pub opening in its stride and offers tea and coffee from mid-morning. Extensive bar food includes vegetarian pasta, shepherd's pie, lasagne, moussaka, sausages and two veg, beef ragoût, chicken chasseur, lamb pissanda and chilli con carne; there is a traditional roast lunch on Sundays.

As well as HMS Belfast and the Tower, Horniman's is close to the London Dungeon in Tooley Street, a grisly exhibition of London past.

SE3
British Oak
109 Old Dover Road

✗ lunchtime

🍺 garden and terrace

🍺 **Courage Best Bitter, Directors Bitter**

The British Oak is a large roadhouse built between the two world wars. It has a dominating claret and cream porticoed frontage, with tiles on the ground floor and an impressive wrought iron balcony above. There are two bars, a vast and spacious saloon and a public that is scarcely any smaller. The saloon has partitions formed by a couple of high-backed settles and there are more settles against the walls, with some small tables and chairs. The windows have curtains and blinds; hanging baskets are suspended from a central ceiling cupola of red, white and pink glass.

The large bar has a mahogany dado with globe lights built into it. The substantial lunchtime menu offers cottage pie, macaroni cheese, lasagne, chilli, chicken curry, scampi, cod, plaice, salads, ploughman's, egg and chips, jacket potatoes, toasties, omelettes, and vegetarian nut cutlets with salad and chips.

The public has a narrow section alongside the bar and then swells into a larger area with an open fire and mantelpiece at the end. To the right of the pub there are a few bench seats on the pavement and French windows in the saloon lead to a large walled beer garden where

🚊 Blackheath/Maze Hill (both a good ten or fifteen minutes' walk)

Places to see: Blackheath

133

barbecues are held in good weather at weekends.

British Oak has naval connections – many proud ships have carried the name – and also royal ones, for Charles I took refuge in a tree (where he enjoyed some good ale and cheese) when he was escaping from the parliamentary "Roundheads". The Blackheath British Oak is a deservedly popular tavern, busy at lunchtimes and evenings and a handy base for visiting the elegant sweep of Blackheath with its parkland and fine houses.

SE5
Phoenix and
Firkin

5 Windsor Walk (Denmark Hill Station)

✗ lunchtime and evening

🍴 seats on pavement

🍺 **Rail Ale, Phoenix Bitter, Dogbolter; guest beers**

🚄 Denmark Hill (reached from Blackfriars: approximately six minutes' journey time).

This is the apotheosis of the Firkins – David Bruce's finest achievement – a large, fun-filled boozer with a splendid vaulted and beamed roof, part of Denmark Hill station: as you climb the stairs from the platforms you catch a whiff of beer being brewed, followed by the clank of glasses and the merry laughter of the drinkers.

The Phoenix is also a cautionary tale about both the stupidity and cupidity of the national beer giants. In 1980 Denmark Hill station was gutted by fire. When British Rail set about rebuilding it, they asked commuters to vote on the amenities they would like to see in the new station. By a heavy majority, the sensible travellers voted for a pub. British Rail put the old station entrance hall out to tender and one after another the beer barons said they were not interested. Then a group of local people, including the film director and writer Terry Jones of Monty Python fame, suggested that David Bruce should be asked to build one of his brewpubs there.

There were obvious problems about building a small brewery alongside a busy railway line but Bruce accepted the challenge and was offered a deal by BR. And then the self-same beer barons who had spurned the opportunity went to court to try and stop Bruce getting a licence for the pub: they were too lethargic and indolent to run a pub there themselves but they were determined to stop competition, even from a pip-squeak like David Bruce. To their eternal credit, the magistrates granted a licence and the Phoenix rose from the ashes.

Because the Phoenix is larger than his other outlets, Bruce was able to give full reign to his concept of the fun-pub. The main bar has tiled and bare-brick walls and lights suspended from the high ceiling along with a large clock made by Potts and Son, acquired from a station in Wales. The walls are decorated with railway memorabilia and such brewing artefacts as hop pockets, the large sacks in which hops are stored. Seats are provided in the shape of old church pews and wooden tables.

A spiral staircase leads up to a balcony with more seats and views of the throngs below. At the far end of the main room a double arch leads to another smaller room that also serves beer but is used mainly as a food servery: a great glass cabinet offers the usual Firkin fare: hot specials plus pies, quiches, salads and giant filled baps. You can take food and drink outside and sit at British Rail benches under a handsome wrought iron canopy.

The usual caveat: the Bruce beers brewed in the cellar are lightly pressurised and are not recognised as "real ale" but the guest beers, such as Shepherd Neame's wonderfully hoppy Kentish bitter, or Marston's Pedigree, are pukka. Whatever you drink, raise your glass to the now-retired David Bruce and his tongue-in-cheek success: the pub's T-shirts with the slogan "Phoenix My Pint I'll Firkin Punch Him" must have the teeth-gnashing big brewers in mind.

SE10
Cutty Sark

Ballast Quay

✗ lunchtime and evening

🍴 terrace

@ upstairs room

🍺 **Draught Bass, Charrington IPA**

Greenwich's waterfront is dominated by the great tea clipper, the Cutty Sark, now laid to rest on the quayside and open to visitors. The pub, despite its name, is not close to the ship. To get to the pub (first called the Union and renamed in honour of the ship) turn right from the ship and walk along the embankment past the handsome buildings of the Royal Naval College, where the likes of Lord Nelson learnt the tricks of the trade, keep going past a seventeenth-century hospital and an ugly twentieth-century power station and then pick up the signs for Ballast Quay.

The pub dominates a small row of houses. It has a stark black and white frontage with the name picked out in white lettering on a large and imposing bowed section that overhangs the entrance. The Cutty Sark was built in 1695 and the Georgian building is now a listed property. There are two floors, both heavy with beams and ships' lamps. The ground floor has bare boards, low ceilings, bare brick walls and an impressive open fire surmounted by a great ship's timber acting as a mantelpiece, with a ship's wheel above it.

Seats and tables are made from old wooden beer casks while the bar is a mix of planks and mahogany pillars. A servery next to the bar offers a wide range of food, the daily dishes chalked on a blackboard. There is a strong sea influence with whitebait, haddock and scampi, plus pies, salads, pastie and chips, sausage, egg and chips, omelettes, garlic mushrooms, and ploughman's.

A short flight of stairs with a wooden balustrade leads up to the first floor: there is no bar here and children are allowed. The two-tiered floor is carpeted, the walls are wood panelled, and there are high-backed settles, wall seats and splendid views over the Thames from the great bow window.

Across the road there are a few benches on the embankment. To the right the broad bend of

🚉 Maze Hill/Greenwich

Places to see: Cutty Sark, Maritime Museum, Naval College, Greenwich Park, home of Sir John Vanbrugh (Maze Hill).

the river serves industry on the near bank whilst on the north side warehouses are being re-fashioned as apartments.

You can get to Greenwich, with its broad parkland and views north over London, the National Maritime Museum and Naval College, by train but the nicest way to come is by river from Westminister Bridge, where there are frequent boats.

Richard I

52 Royal Hill

✗ lunchtime

🍺 beer garden and seats on pavement

🍺 **Young Bitter, Special Bitter, Winter Warmer**

🚆 Greenwich

This small and welcoming Young's pub is reached up a pleasantly climbing and winding street, disfigured only by the hideous New Brutalism town hall at the bottom. The pub has a brown and cream fascia with seats made of old logs on the forecourt between two bow windows. It is known locally as "Tolly's" and old photos inside show the pub when it was owned by the Ipswich brewery of Tollemache, which later merged with its Suffolk rival Cobbold to form Tolly Cobbold. Tolly had a depot in Walthamstow, East London, to supply the capital with beer.

Now it is a Young's house but little changed, I suspect, from the days of its former owners. It has two bars. The saloon has bare boards, half-panelled walls and flock wallpaper, wooden bench tables, captain's chairs and old settles in the bow window. There are many old prints of Greenwich on the walls and the low-beamed ceiling is painted cream. The spacious public bar is plainer, with cream painted walls and a few small, round tables and stools.

At the rear of the saloon, French windows lead to a pleasant beer garden with wooden benches and chairs. Lunchtime food is simple pub fare: steak pie and chips, sausages, beans and chips, egg and chips, and rolls and sandwiches.

The Richard I is one of those no-frills pubs

where you instantly feel at home. It is on the fringe of Greenwich proper and is a good spot for a rest and a drink between the station and the town.

SE16
Mayflower
117 Rotherhithe Street

✖ lunchtime and evening; separate restaurant

🍴 riverside terrace

🍺 **Draught Bass, Charrington IPA**

The Mayflower was first called the Spreadeagle and Crown; the name was changed to commemorate the spot on the Thames where the founding fathers left in the Mayflower in 1611 on their voyage to North America. The tavern was built in the sixteenth century, rebuilt in the eighteenth and sensitively given a face-lift in the 1960s to retain its original atmosphere. It stands in a street of social upheaval, where old warehouses are being hammered into riverside homes for Cynthia and Charles Upwardly-Mobile. It is a small, two-storeyed building with lattice windows, flower boxes on the first-floor window ledges and a dormer window in the roof.

There is a powerful nautical feel to the interior, with old ships' timbers around the bar, black beams on the low ceiling, black-winged settles, black tables and little alcoves where you half expect to find jolly jack tars smoking clay pipes over their mugs of ale. There is a model of the Mayflower and other ships of the period and ships' lamps on and above the bar, while a small cabinet behind the bar has a display of sailors' rope knots.

At the rear of the saloon, a couple of steps take you to a section overlooking the river. On the wall to the right the pub's owners have displayed the lengthy and fascinating will and last testament of the splendidly named Beatrice Brewing. Written in copper-plate writing in 1697, the will was bequeathed to the pub.

An outside terrace has been built on river piles. I get a slightly eery feeling sitting there high above the river, wondering what went through

⊖ Rotherhithe

Places to see: St Mary's Church

the minds of the God-fearing folk who set out in 1611 on that daunting and perilous journey to the Americas.

The first floor, up narrow and ricketty stairs, is used as a restaurant in the evening. There is a lunchtime food counter offering soup, pasta, chilli and rice, lasagne, filled baps and jacket potatoes. You can eat the food there or take it downstairs.

I forgot to buy a stamp when I was last there. The Mayflower has the unique right for a pub to sell postage stamps, a right granted originally for the convenience of sailors. Just a few yards from the pub is the lovely church of St Mary's, built by Wren.

CROYDON
Dog and Bull

24 Surrey Street

✘ liver sausage rolls

◖ **Young Bitter, Special Bitter, Winter Warmer**

Croydon is as far south as you can go in the county of Greater London before you fall off the edge into Surrey. Croydonians do not consider themselves to be Londoners and were dragged complaining into the new county in the 1970s. It is a town with its own distinctive history and it has one of the most remarkable and unspoilt pubs you are likely to find.

Ye Dog and Bull, to give it its full title, stands in a small and raucous street with an open-air market. The stall owners and street traders use the pub, which in the special shorthand of CAMRA's Good Beer Guide is described as "basic". That means no frills, no concessions to creature comforts: it is an alehouse short and simple, not a place for the faint-hearted, the vicar or the maiden aunt.

As it is just a place for serving beer, it does so with remarkable facility. It is the closest thing to a Scottish "beer shop": however packed it is, merely hold up the necessary number of fingers – but in the Dog and Bull be careful about displaying just two fingers, as the clientele might get the wrong message – or shout your

⊨ East Croydon

Places to see: Surrey Street market

order and the pints come frothing into the glasses and on to the bar top.

You have to duck and weave through the market stalls to get into the small building, with an inn sign showing a dog worrying a ferocious looking beast, recalling the time when the sport (sic) of bull-baiting existed. There are scuffed, weather-beaten doors at either end that take you into a front bar dominated by a great circular serving area topped by a gantry holding empty glasses. The floors are bare boards and there are a few benches built into the wall below the front windows with leaded interpretations of both a dog and a bull. The wood-panelling along the walls has seen better times and they are decorated with old prints that have no particular theme and the obligatory coloured portrait of the Queen Mother pulling a pint of Young's Special.

The customers are mainly market workers, the men in flat caps, the women in aprons, who dash in for a quick pint and put the world to rights with a rough humour and views that would make even Mrs Thatcher blanch. An open doorway to the rear of the bar is topped by a pair of bull's horns. Inside there are a few bench seats, a boarded-up fireplace – they can't have the customers getting warm – and a rear window with bars: "to stop double-glazing salesmen from getting in" one regular explained.

The food is rudimentary and confined as far as I could see to liver sausage rolls: if you are hungry, go to the excellent fish restaurant across the road. But don't avoid the Dog and Bull. Not only does it serve immaculate beer but it remains as a now rare example of the basic boozer designed for hard-working, down-to-earth people. The day Youngs turn it into a wine bar called Johnnies I shall emigrate.

SWI
Buckingham Arms

62 Petty France

✗ lunchtime and evening; separate restaurant

🍺 **Young Bitter, Special Bitter, Winter Warmer**

Store the name of the Buckingham Arms in your memory bank: if you have to wait for a little blue book (or a Europass) at the Passport Office in Petty France you will be in desperate need of nourishment. The Buckingham is ideally placed to provide vital sustenance for your frayed nerves. The pleasant exterior has a portrait of the Duke (of whom more anon), small bowed and mullioned windows and a recessed tiled entrance. A separate entrance leads up to the first-floor restaurant.

The interior is richly carpeted, with a long bar running almost the length of the building and at a right angle to the street. A narrow passage by the bar has a ledge along the wall where customers can rest elbows, food and drink. The walls are bare brick and tiled, with a few engravings of the area. Beyond the bar and beneath a wood-and-glass canopy the room swells into a larger area packed with tables and chairs and in great demand at lunchtime. A food servery to the right offers such unusual dishes for London as haggis and neaps (the traditional Scots meal of mince boiled in sheep gut with mashed turnips), plus burgers, sausages, quiche and ploughman's.

A fascinating collection of Toby jugs is stacked behind the bar while there are portraits of the Duke and his family towards the rear of the pub. The Duke (1592 to 1628) was a confidant of both James I and Charles I; his arrogance and greed were in part responsible for the tensions that led to the English Civil War between the parliamentary party of Oliver Cromwell and the supporters of the monarch. The Duke became a highly unpopular figure and was assassinated by a naval officer.

The pub named in his dubious honour is a good base not only for the Passport Office but also for visiting Westminster Abbey and the Houses of Parliament.

⊖ St James's Park

Places to see: Westminster Abbey, Houses of Parliament

Morpeth Arms

58 Millbank

✗ lunchtime and evening

🍴 seats on pavement

🍺 **Young Bitter, Special Bitter, Winter Warmer**

This small and beautifully-appointed pub is on a corner of Millbank with the Thames across the road. There are seats and tables with parasols on the pavement. Inside the elegant one-bar pub there is a small and solid two-tier oak bar, with glasses on the first tier and the top one packed with old bound copies of the Law Journal (to help the management bone up on the licensing laws, perhaps), plus stone jars and other bric-à-brac. A great domed lamp is suspended from the ceiling and there are comfortable green-padded settles along the wall, with tables and chairs set aside for diners.

The section of bar close to Millbank is spacious, with old photos on the lincrusta walls and a fine engraved glass mirror next to the food servery, then the room narrows into a passageway that runs alongside the bar. The pub gleams and sparkles and has a pleasing mix of customers, with cheerful Cockneys from the side streets and visitors to the Tate Gallery, the capital's foremost gallery for twentieth century art, founded by the sugar refiner Sir Henry Tate, which is just along the embankment.

In common with several Young's pubs, the Morpeth Arms serves the Irish stout Beamish, which is featured in one of the many imaginative dishes supplied by the food servery: beef in Beamish pie, chicken chasseur, lamb curry, smoked mackerel salad, pizza, quiche, ploughman's, salads, with sherry trifle to follow if you

🚉 Vauxhall

⊖ Vauxhall

Places to see: Tate Gallery

have room.

Star Tavern

6 Belgrave Mews West

✗ lunchtime

🍺 **Fuller Chiswick Bitter, London Pride, ESB**

The Star is one of Fuller's most popular pubs, a delightful Georgian building in a cobbled mews off the elegant sweep of Belgrave Square. The three-storey pub rises above an archway leading into the mews. The name "STAR TAVERN." complete with full stop is picked out of the brickwork just below the flat roof. There is no formal pub sign, just a large star suspended from a metal bracket above the entrance. Two steps lead up to the narrow doorway. Inside you are immediately faced by the small bar area and beyond a corridor and stairs that lead up to the first floor.

The main ground-floor room runs to the left of the bar. It is comfortable and welcoming, a mix of coffee shop and gentlemen's club. There are tables, chairs and *chaises longues*, a carpeted floor and artefacts of the imperial tea and coffee trade with the East on the dark green walls. A gilt Fuller's brewery sign is placed above a large wall mirror and globe lights and revolving fans are suspended from the ceiling. A real fire adds a welcoming winter blaze.

The stylish upstairs lounge also has an open fire, a tiny bar in the left-hand corner and great windows that give excellent views of the mews. Pub lunches offer sirloin steak, barbecue chicken, gammon steak and vegetarian quiche, all served with chips and salads.

The name star often has a religious theme, referring either to the Star of Bethlehem or the Virgin Mary. From the seventeenth century a sixteen-pointed star featured in the arms of the Worshipful Company of Innholders but the star outside the Belgrave tavern has just five points and, given the tea trade artefacts inside, may be based on the insignia of the Star of India.

⊖ Knightsbridge/Hyde Park Corner

Westminster Arms

7 Storeys Gate

✘ lunchtime and evening;
separate wine bar and
restaurants

🍴 seats on pavement

🍺 Arkell Best Bitter; Brakspear
Bitter; Eldridge Pope Dorset
Original IPA; King & Barnes
Sussex Bitter; Marston
Pedigree

⊖ St James's Park/Westminster

Places to see: Houses of
Parliament, Westminster
Abbey

The Westminister Arms is so popular with Members of Parliament that the pub has a division bell: if the people's representatives are needed for a vote in the Commons the bell rings in the pub to summon them back to their duties. When I had to record an interview with an MP who was keen on his ale he said: "Don't come to the House – the beer's lousy. I'll see you in the Westminster Arms." It was good thinking on his part, even though I had almost to stick the microphone down his throat in order to get his voice on tape above the hubbub in the bar.

The pub has a tall and impressive frontage, with a couple of wooden benches on the pavement. Through the door, there is a tiny alcove to the left – where I did the interview – and then the spacious bar with the counter against the right-hand wall. The walls are wood-panelled and some of the windows have attractive stained glass.

If the ground-floor bar is too crowded for comfort, then take the stairs to the attractive first-floor lounge. There is a wine bar in the basement and a restaurant next door. Pub food includes home-made steak and kidney pie, Wiltshire gammon and chips, vegetarian quiche, ham and mushroom pie and ploughman's. The pub is a genuine free house, which means that the range of beer is liable to change.

SW4
Olde Windmill

South Side, Clapham Common

✘ lunchtime and evening;
separate restaurant

🍴 beer garden

🛏

🍺 Young Bitter, Special Bitter,
Winter Warmer

Ye Olde Windmill is not that old. It is a Victorian pub built on the site of an earlier coaching inn next to the house of Florance Young, mother of the founder of Young's brewery. It is a handsome pub, one of the brewery's most popular, with the record for selling more beer than any other of the company's outlets – more than a million pints a year. It lies back from the main road in a cul-de-sac and the small exterior belies the size of the interior, which is broken up into several small and intimate areas. The interior is brightly lit thanks to a profusion of windows, some with attractive stained glass. The main room has a domed ceiling and wood-panelled walls, decorated with old prints, many with a windmill theme.

There is a plentiful supply of tables, chairs and green upholstered wall benches. The semi-circular bar serves the front section and a smaller rear one which includes a large nineteeth-century print showing the Prince Consort, the Duke of Wellington and Lord Palmerston celebrating in style in the original inn in 1863 after a good day at the races. This was in the time when the inn was on a coaching route that took in Epsom Downs, the racecourse where the Derby is staged.

To the right is another large lounge with its own bar counter and bright furnishings. A large servery at the back of this room offers such excellent fare as cock a leekie soup, moussaka, quiche, vegetarian harvest pie and ploughman's. A door from the lounge leads into a spacious garden with tables and benches and a colonnaded shelter. A second beer garden is situated at the other end of the pub.

The first inn on the site was built in 1665 by Thomas Crenshaw, a miller with a windmill on the common. The modern pub maintains the coaching inn tradition by offering accommodation in an extension block with thirteen rooms. The common is a fine place for walks and there are often fairs, including a great annual jamboree when the high spot is the appearance of the Young's brewery dray horses.

⊖ Clapham Common

Places to see: Clapham Common

SW6
White Horse

1 Parsons Green

✖ lunchtime and evening; weekend breakfasts

🍺 outside drinking area

🎷 weekend live jazz

🍺 **Charrington IPA, Draught Bass and M&B Highgate Mild and regular guest beers, including Traquair House Ale in winter**

The White Horse is the centre of the small and vibrant community of Parsons Green, with a wealth of red-bricked Victorian housing and a good mix of older residents and new arrivals in the form of writers, journalists and people who say "I'm in television, actually". The pub faces the green and you can catch a tantalising glimpse of it from the Underground, its name picked out on a cream cornice that rises above the buildings (including two other pubs) closer to the station.

The smart exterior has cream and red-brick on the first floor, rising to a tall and imposing cornice at the right-hand side. There is a small cast-iron balustrade above the ground floor, old coaching lamps, hanging baskets, with pine doors and marbled brickwork below. There is no pub sign but a white horse is painted on the fascia above the main entrance.

In front and overlooking the green is a spacious terraced beer garden with many white-painted cast-iron tables and chairs, screened by trees planted in large wooden "pots".

Inside, the pub is vast and spacious. The enormous, ceiling-to-floor windows and deep button-leather sofas and wall settles give the pub the feel of an elegant brasserie. The walls are half-panelled with a few prints as decoration. There are sensibly placed "leaning posts" – slim pillars with circular rests where customers can place glasses and plates. The great galleried horseshoe bar has a frieze of hops running along it. In the far right hand corner by a window there is a small raised area where live jazz is played at the weekend. Close to it, a handsome marble fireplace belts out welcoming heat in winter.

Further round the corner, at the extremity of the bar, a large servery dispenses generous portions of food, ranging from gargantuan breakfasts at the weekend, roast lunch on

⊖ Parsons Green

Sunday, and such weekday lunchtime and evening meals as mushroom soup, egg mayonnaise, pâté, Mexican pie, sausages, beans and chips, and liver and bacon. A section with cream-painted bare-brick walls has been set aside for diners.

Although the pub is owned by Bass's Charrington subsidiary, it allows the tenants considerable leeway in the beers on offer. As well as the Bass ales listed above, a guest beer, such as Brakspear Bitter or Bateman's from Lincolnshire is always available.

Every winter there is a festival of old ales, such as porters, barley wines and Christmas ales, and the pub is the only London outlet for Traquair House Ale, brewed in a stately home in the Scottish borders by the Laird of Traquair. The house is the oldest inhabited house in Scotland, was host to both Mary Queen of Scots and Prince Charles Edward Stuart, and is the only licensed stately house brewery in the country.

The winter festival is organised by the energetic Mark Dorber, an enthusiastic devotee of real ale. He is so concerned by the decline of the London pub that he was surprised I had managed to find so many for this guide. "I can only think of ten really good London pubs these days," he said. I think there are a few more than that, but the White Horse is high on the perfectionist's list. It is a genuine community local where enormous care is taken over the quality of beer, food and wine – the pub was nominated Wine Pub of the Year in 1988.

SW8
Surprise

16 Southville, off Wandsworth Road

✘ lunchtime snacks

🍴 patio

🍺 **Young Bitter, Special Bitter, Winter Warmer**

🚉 Wandsworth Road/
⊖ Stockwell

A surprise indeed. This part of Lambeth is not famed for the quality of its pubs but you turn off the main road into a short cul-de-sac and this small gem of a pub is at the end with a pleasant outlook over undulating Larkhall Park. The inn sign shows a ram – the Young's brewery mascot – butting a startled brewer but the origin of the name is almost certainly nautical, for many ships bear the name. For example, a frigate called the Surprise took Napoleon Bonaparte's body from St Helena to France.

The Lambeth Surprise has hanging baskets decking out the exterior and, alongside the entrance to the park, a small beer garden with trellis work and climbing plants. You get a genuine, unforced London welcome when you enter the small front bar with its half-panelled walls and a carpeted floor. A corridor leads to an area at the rear with black leather-and-wood seats and a log fire in a stone surround decorated with horse brasses. Beyond is a games room with darts and a pool table.

The pub is popular with locals from the surrounding estates and students from the great sprawl of the Polytechnic of the South Bank in the main road. Rolls and sandwiches are provided lunchtime.

SW13
Bull's Head

373 Lonsdale Road

✘ lunchtime and evening; separate restaurant

🎵 live jazz

🍺 **Young Bitter, Special Bitter, Winter Warmer**

🚉 Barnes Bridge

You don't have to enjoy modern jazz to visit the Bull's Head at Barnes, but it does help, as the music from the room at the back of the pub tends to permeate in muffled form the rest of the building. The Bull's Head is a superb and stately tavern in its own right overlooking the Thames – on good days you can take your drink and sit on the embankment wall. The three-storey exterior is impressive, with a pillared entrance, iron-work balconies below the first and top floors, the pub's name picked out of the brickwork of the roof, and a most unusual dormered steeple that is reminiscent of a Kentish oast house.

There are two large bars inside. The main lounge has a large island servery and many side alcoves. Meals are served in a separate restaurant and the excellent bar food includes soup with crusty bread, a pasta dish of the day, a lunchtime roast beef carvery, hot beef sandwiches, home-made pies, salads and sandwiches. The cheerful public bar has a dartboard.

Jazz is staged every evening and weekend lunchtimes in the large music room and such is the fame of the pub that top players from the US and Europe perform there alongside British musicians. The entire pub pulsates to the beat of big bands at weekends. It costs around £3 for admittance – the charge depends on the quality of the musicians. Future concerts are chalked on the wall behind the players. The performances are enthusiastic and the cost is minimal: if you went to a jazz club in the West End you would be charged half an arm and both legs and wouldn't get change from a fiver for a glass of insipid lager. At the Bull's Head you get quality entertainment on the cheap – and Young's ale for good measure.

Details of performances: 01-876 5241

SW15
White Lion

14 Putney High Street

✗ lunchtime and evening

🍺 Arkell Kingsdown Ale; Boddingtons Bitter; Brakspear Bitter; Darley Dark Mild; Greene King Abbot Ale; Ward Sheffield Best Bitter; Vaux Samson

⊖ Putney

The White Lion has a commanding position close to the junction of the High Street and Putney Bridge. It is an imposing five-storey building with a brown stone ground floor façade, surmounted by white nymphs whose raised arms hold up the third floor. The pub dates from 1887 and the sizeable interior is divided into many small nooks and crannies with the adroit use of wood partitions and leaded windows. A vast and meandering bar runs almost the whole length of the pub and has as its centrepiece an intriguing collection of ties.

There are comfortable settles and banquettes in alcoves and a large open fire with a carved wood mantel in a large seating area at the back of the building. Old prints on the walls include several interesting nineteenth-century indentures; the walls themselves are half-panelled, with tasteful brown patterned wallpaper above. There are fans slowly revolving below the wonderfully moulded ceilings.

A good and imaginative range of food is supplied from a servery towards the rear of the pub, with such dishes as braised steak, pasta capaletti and salad, sausage in French bread, chicken, chips and peas, quiche, salads and ploughman's.

The White Lion is another of the Vaux group's recent London acquisitions, along with Crockers and the Princess Louise (see entries). They seem to have a fascination for late Victorian buildings and the White Lion is a worthy partner for the better-known outlets in central and north London. Vaux should be congratulated for serving a dark mild – a beer style not often seen in the capital. I hope it is still on offer when you visit the pub.

SW18
Alma
499 York Road

✗ lunchtime and evening; separate wine bar

⊄ **Young Bitter, Special Bitter, Winter Warmer**

The Alma could also be known as "*L'hôtel de la gare*" for this spacious and extraordinary building opposite Wandsworth Town station has been given a touch of the French *brasserie* by Young's brewery. Wandsworth is the home of Young's fine Victorian brewery and the company's idiosyncratic humour dominates the town: a poster on a corner of the brewery tells drivers caught in the snarl of the South Circular Road that the company "has been going round the bend since 1831".

The Alma vies with Crockers in Maida Vale (see entry) as one of the finest *fin de siècle* pubs in London, with a diagonal brown, black and white tiled floor, engraved glass windows and screens, an enormous mahogany island bar, wooden pillars and gleaming, polished wooden stairs sweeping up to the first floor. An impressive old clock in an iron frame is suspended above the bar. There is an abundance of splendid mirrors with engraved flower motifs and great globe lights are suspended from the ceiling.

The French touch may upset some purists: I note that the Alma appeared in the 1988 Good Beer Guide but was dropped from the following edition. I find the atmosphere a delight: there are newspapers on the bar, bikes against the wall and the type of authentic old table football game – with the players manipulated by rods – that I have often seen in bars in northern France. Bar food, as you would expect, includes beef, cheese and ham baguettes, croque monsieur, onion soup and Mediterranean prawns plus steaks and sea fish crumble. A wine bar at the back of the enormous saloon has old railway posters, and a cold buffet laid out on a table.

The Alma's exterior has an abundance of green tiles and hanging baskets. The pub, fittingly, is named after the battle in the Crimea in 1854 when the British and French armies united to defeat the Russians.

➤ Wandsworth Town

Crane

14 Armoury Way (corner of Dormay Street)

✗ lunchtime; separate restaurant

🍺 garden; seats on pavement

🍺 **Young Bitter, Special Bitter, Winter Warmer**

I'm a country boy at heart and I fell for the Crane many years ago when I crossed – at some risk to my person – the South Circular Road, entered the small, cottage-style pub and felt that I could be a hundred miles away in a country inn surrounded by woods and fields rather than on one of London's main arterial roads.

The Crane has the old fashioned pleasure of two bars, a public and a saloon, both low-ceilinged and divided by a wooden partition. The public bar is tiny, with half-leaded windows and an open fire. The saloon, running at right angles round the small bar counter, has horse brasses on the walls, and photos of the Young's dray horses. Framed front pages of the local newspaper, the Wandsworth Borough News, give fascinating accounts of World War Two and other ancient events.

There are a few seats on the pavement, but you may need ear muffs, a beer garden at the rear and a small upstairs restaurant. Bar lunches include a daily special, such as pork curry and rice (an extremely rare dish from the East) and sandwiches.

There isn't much more to say: the Crane is just a delightful, unspoilt street-corner boozer that the harsh modern world has fortunately passed by. The pub is reputed to be haunted, but not by a dissatisfied customer.

⇥ Wandsworth Town

Grapes

39 Fairfield Street (corner of Wandsworth High Street)

✗ lunchtime

🍺 beer garden

🍺 **Young Bitter, Special Bitter, Winter Warmer**

You can tell that the Grapes serves good beer for it is packed at lunchtime with workers in their brown overalls from Young's brewery: the brewery is at the end of Fairfield Street and there is a heady aroma of malted barley and hops in the air. (Some of the brewery staff, I must mention in passing, were drinking *lager*, but I leave it to the management to deal with this sad dereliction of duty.)

The pub is a splendid little local, small, cheerful and with fast, efficient and welcoming bar staff. The single room is served by a large horseshoe island bar. The walls are half or fully wood-panelled, and there is flock wallpaper, a carpeted floor and comfortable green leather wall seats and stools. A bunch of hops hang behind the bar, testimony to fact that Youngs, unlike some purveyors of bland beers, still use the little plant in their beverages. The doors have engraved glass and the pump handles on the bar have an unusual engraved wood pattern.

The area in front of the bar nearest the

entrance is packed and jostling but there are smaller and quieter sections to the side. I was much taken with a tiny area closest to the main road. With its slightly faded settees, oval and rectangular mirrors built into wood frames and lamps, vases and statuettes, it is powerfully reminiscent of a parlour in a working-class house in the days before formica and plastic wood destroyed such old-world charm.

The Grapes has a beer garden to the side of the pub which is used by families with young children. Lunchtime food is simple pub fare served in generous portions: steak and kidney pie, chicken and chips, burgers and sandwiches.

As the brewery is close at hand it should be mentioned that visits round this amazing and delightful place can be arranged, but there is a long waiting list to see the Victorian beam engine that once supplied all the power, the traditional vats and coppers, the stables with the dray horses, and the ram mascot. Phone 870 0141 for details.

🚄 Wandsworth Town

Places to see: Young's brewery

Ship

41 Jew's Row

✖ lunchtime and evening; summer barbecue; occasional floating restaurant

🍴 garden and terrace

☺

🍺 **Young Bitter, Special Bitter, Winter Warmer**

The Ship is a hidden delight in an unpromising position. You have to turn off the busy Warple Way, turn right and keep going round a bus garage and you come to Jew's Way. At the end, just before you fall into the Thames, is the Ship, offering an amazing contrast in styles. The first bar you come to is the public, a simple and slightly down-at-heel room with bare boards, half-panelled pine walls, an old kitchen range to the right and a large photograph of a sea-going clipper.

A passage to the left of the bar takes you into the saloon, which has been adventurously extended into a large conservatory, with leather sofas, wooden tables, a pianola and a frieze of hops above the bar. There is more to come: beyond the conservatory is a two-tiered patio and courtyard, with plants clambering up trellis-work. The ground is partly cobbled and there are benches, tables and tubs of flowers. If the seats are occupied – highly likely in warm weather – take your food and drink and sit on the wall overlooking the river. A Thames barge is moored alongside and is sometimes available both as a restaurant and for cruises.

To the left facing the river is yet a further part of the beer garden, with a large barbecue area offering a wide array of food, cooked to order. You can choose from burgers, sausages, trout, steaks and chops. Food inside the Ship includes a half-pint of fresh prawns, tomato and bean soup, turkey and vegetable pies, salads and cheese platter.

If it were not for the nautical connections, the Ship would be better blessed with that famous old pub name Who'd a Thought It, for who would have thought that such a fine alehouse existed at the rear of Wandsworth bus garage? Seek it out.

≛ Wandsworth Town

Spread Eagle

71 Wandsworth High Street

✗ lunchtime

🍺 **Young Bitter, Special Bitter, Winter Warmer**

≛ Wandsworth Town

Places to see: Wandsworth Town Hall

I felt that "sumptuous" did not do the Spread Eagle justice and looked the word up in my synonym finder. I think "priceless, inestimable, opulent, lavish, dazzling, imposing, palatial, august, majestic, awe-inspiring" begin to give the feel of the place. It is one of the finest Victorian drinking places in London, a museum of engraved glass in mahogany frames. The public bar must surely take the prize for the best of its kind; such rooms tend to be plain and no-nonsense, set aside for working chaps in their overalls. But the public bar of the Spread Eagle continues the opulent theme, with yet more engraved glass and a vast counter.

The saloon has an array of old prints and photos, a large and sonorous Kilburn clock, comfortable wall seats, hanging baskets suspended from the ceiling, and wooden casks and jugs on a high shelf. Beyond the great curved sweep of the bar there is a lounge on two levels, with brown button furnishings, modern prints on the walls and a piano.

Lunches include roast chicken and two veg, chilli and rice, and cauliflower cheese and salad. A sign says "late breakfasts" and presumably are sold to people so overcome by the place, with its high moulded ceilings and airy elegance, that they refuse to leave at closing time and are found asleep on the deep wall seats in the morning.

Opposite the pub is Wandsworth town hall and civic centre, a splendid example of 1920s municipal architecture.

RICHMOND
Orange Tree

45 Kew Road

✘ lunchtime and evening; separate restaurant

🍴 seats on pavement

☺ in restaurant

♔ theatre

🍺 **Young Bitter, Special Bitter, Winter Warmer**

🚂 Richmond

⊖ Richmond

Places to see: the riverside and Richmond Park

As you turn into Richmond from the London road the Orange Tree is the first pub you see; if you come by train, it is just across the road from the station, to the right. It has an imposing frontage, with a marbled ground floor, an orange tree motif engraved in one window and two enormous coaching lamps over the entrance. There are two red-brick storeys above with a dormered roof and a cupola on the right hand corner. The name of the pub, thought to commemorate the arrival of the orange tree in Britain, not the House of Orange from the Netherlands, is embellished on the left hand side wall and the inn sign atop a pillar on the pavement — which has a few wooden tables and benches — shows an orange tree flowering in a large pot.

There is a restaurant in the cellar with bare brick walls and a tiled floor. On the ground floor a large island bar serves a spacious lounge with a carpeted floor: the entrance is marked "public bar" and "saloon" but there is now just one room. It has an embossed ceiling with a pattern of fruit and plants, coaching prints and paintings of the "Seven Ages of Man" by Henry Stacy Marks, which were presented to the Green Room Theatre Club in the Orange Tree in 1921.

The furnishings and decorations are impressively florid. The ochre-coloured walls are above brown lincrusta; wood pillars stand on the red carpet and are also built into the walls. Similar pillars support little glass-laden gantries above the mirror-faced mahogany bar. There are no fewer than three open coal and log fires; the one at the far end of the saloon is set in a splendid wood-pillared mantel.

Food at the bar includes rolls and sandwiches, scampi, and liver and bacon. In the cellar you can choose from a daily menu that may include taramosalata, pâté, soup and smoked mackerel, followed by beef and vegetable pie, lasagne, rack of lamb, lamb casserole, beef salads and smoked trout salad.

The upstairs theatre still flourishes on the first floor and occasionally its highly professional productions are transferred to the West End. When I visited in the autumn of 1988 Tom Courtenay was starring there and a well-known television actor was walking up and down outside the pub, parading his profile.

Richmond is one of London's most charming and elegant areas. There are fine houses in streets that slip down to the Thames, a handsome theatre on the Green, and Richmond Park, where you may not shoot the deer as they belong to the monarch.

WEST LONDON

The Dove. Hammersmith

W2
Archery Tavern
Bathurst Street

✖ lunchtime and evening

🍴 seats on pavement

🍺 **Adnams Bitter; Arkell Best Bitter; Fuller London Pride; Marston Pedigree; Tetley Bitter; Wadworth 6X**

This cheery and welcoming little pub is in a pedestrian precinct just a few yards from Bayswater Road and the vast open spaces of Hyde Park, one of London's most famous parklands enlivened by the soap box orators at Hyde Park Corner. The pub was originally the Crown Tavern but was renamed to mark the fact that it was on the site of the archery ground owned by the Royal Toxopholite Society in the nineteenth century. A toxopholite is literally "a lover of the bow" and members of the society gathered there to play the upper-class version of darts with their bows and arrows.

As you would expect, the pub is decked out with many old prints and memorabilia depicting the toxopholites at their pursuit (I suspect that if you asked someone in modern London if he was a toxopholite you might get a dusty answer). The large horseshoe bar serves a long and narrow room to one side and a smaller one to the right. There are half-panelled walls and settles and stools, a dark green ceiling and added colour from pot plants.

The range of beer is imaginative, as is the food; devilled chicken, moussaka, and beef stew with dumplings (a rare sighting of a traditional London dish). There are tables and chairs on the pavement. The pub is a good base for Hyde Park and Marble Arch and is close to the western end of Oxford Street.

⊖ Lancaster Gate

Places to see: Hyde Park, Marble Arch, Oxford Street

W4
City Barge
27 Strand on the Green

✖ lunchtime and evening; separate restaurant

🍴 seats on towpath

🍺 **Courage Best Bitter, Directors Bitter**

The oldest part of this fine old riverside pub dates from 1484 and was so named because the ceremonial barge of the Lord Mayor of London was moored alongside. The building was badly damaged during the wartime "Blitz" and was carefully and painstakingly restored by Courage when peace returned. The old part is made up of two tiny rooms with low ceilings; it has flood protection doors in case the Thames reaches beyond its usual level and the fireplace in the Old Bar is raised above the quarry-tiled floor for fear the river should pour in. There is a bowed and ancient overmantel, copper-topped tables and wooden wall benches, ochre-painted walls, a corner cupboard containing miniature bottles and a collection of mugs kept behind latticed glass. The second small room serves as the pub's restaurant.

In sharp distinction, the New Bar, a more recent addition, has carpets, lots of maritime prints and signs, central pillars with elbow rests and a few tables and chairs. Behind this bar is a charming conservatory with pot plants and ferns, cast iron tables and wicker-work chairs. In summer weather many customers prefer to flock on to the towpath and sit on the wall to watch the river flow by.

Good pub fare includes crayfish, mussels, smoked mackerel salad, moussaka, lasagne, home-made steak and kidney pie, salads and ploughman's.

⚡ Gunnersbury

W6
Dove

19 Upper Mall

✗ lunchtime

🍺 terrace

🍺 **Fuller London Pride, ESB**

An ancient riverside alehouse long favoured by the literati; William Morris lived next door and Graham Greene and Ernest Hemingway found it a congenial place for a drop. It is hard to imagine such a hairy-chested all-American boy as Hemingway drinking London bitter, but no doubt he considered the pub a clean, well-lighted place. The building dates back to the reign of Charles II and was bought by Fuller, Smith and Turner of Chiswick in 1796. The names of famous customers appear on a panel above the fireplace, flanked by drawings by the caricaturist James Gillray. The present building is only half its original size. The other half became a riverside retreat for Prince Augustus Frederick, the Duke of Sussex (*mein Gott!*) and the sixth son of George III.

⊖ Ravenscourt Park

The main bar offers not only history but exceptionally good lunches dispensed from a glass-fronted servery; you can choose from home-made quiche, sausage and beans, cauli-flower cheese, shepherd's pie, chilli con carne, fish pie, pork Stroganoff and taramosalata with pitta bread. The bar leads on to a partly-covered terrace with an old grapevine and steps down to a larger flagstoned area with teak tables and fine views over the river.

The quiet and homely second bar has wood-panelled walls and wall seats, copper-topped tables, old advertising signs on the walls and photographs of the pub down the ages, plus the manuscript of "Rule, Britannia!", the "alterna-tive" national anthem; its author, James Thom-son, died of a fever in an upper room of the

Dove. His vulgarly jingoist tune brings me out in a sweat.

W8
Britannia

I Allen Street

✗ lunchtime and evening; separate restaurant

🍽 Beer garden

🍺 **Young Bitter, Special Bitter, Winter Warmer**

You get two pubs for the price of one in this happy-go-lucky Young's house a few yards from Kensington High Street. As you enter it seems you are in a pleasant and traditional two-bar pub. Public bar and saloon bar are divided by a wood-and-glass partition and both are served by a large horseshoe bar. The walls are wood-panelled almost to the ceiling and there are a

Vines, ferns and food in the Dove, Hammersmith

few settles and small seats built into the bowed and mullioned windows.

And then comes the surprise. I would have missed it but for a call of nature. At the back of the saloon, the small pre-war pub suddenly blossoms into a spacious and modern room. You feel you have stepped from a time machine as you go down a couple of steps into the airy lounge with its bright furnishings and a clever design that creates several smaller and intimate sections. Facing you is a large bar and a food servery offering quiche, ploughman's, salads, pies and a hot dish of the day at lunchtime.

The acclaimed restaurant has such appetising dishes as steak and kidney pie cooked in Beamish stout, gammon steak, pork chops in red wine, plaice and chips, and salmon. There is a pleasant beer garden to the left of the pub. Three bars, a restaurant and a beer garden – good value for money and a good base for visiting the southern end of Hyde Park, Kensington Gardens, with its statue of Peter Pan, the world's most famous department store – Harrods – and the Royal Albert Hall and Albert Memorial.

⊖ High Street Kensington

Places to see: Harrods, Royal Albert Hall and Albert Memorial, Kensington Gardens

W9
Warrington Hotel

93 Warrington Crescent

✗ lunchtime

🍺 Arkell Best Bitter; Brakspear Special; Fuller London Pride, ESB; Young Special

⊖ Warwick Avenue

Just when you thought Crockers on the other side of the Edgware Road was the most amazing drinking place in the capital, you step from North to West London and find yourself in a place to make a bishop blush. The main claim to fame of this vast and ornate building with some fine *Art Nouveau* tiling is that it was once both a brothel and a building owned by the holier-than-thou Church of England. They say they didn't know about the seedy goings-on there but if you are the biggest landlord in Britain there is fair chance that you will have the odd knocking-shop or two under your ecclesiastical belt.

Needless to say, nothing unseemly or ungodly goes on in the Warrington these days, which

162

despite its name, no longer offers accommodation. The entrance hall is a superb blend of pillars and walls covered with *Art Nouveau* tiles and a fine mosaic floor decked out with wrought-iron lamps. Further in, the enormous bar has a marble top and a canopy with some slightly naughty murals above.

There are more marble pillars and a superb fireplace; on a shelf above the fire stands an empty Champagne bottle, left to commemorate the last (of many) consumed by that legendary star of the London music hall, Marie Lloyd. Beyond the main lounge is a public bar, which rises above the general level of a darts-and-dominoes tap room with an impressive fireplace, etched glass and ornate ceiling.

If you dare venture up the sweep of the marble stairs you come to the first-floor room now used for functions. The rather risqué murals suggest that in days gone by the room was used for events rather more exotic than stag nights or press receptions. It was fortunate that the Church of England's rent collector never strayed far from the bar.

Good lunchtime food in the Warrington does not include poached curate's egg but you can tuck into such tasty home-cooked fare as chilli con carne, lasagne, shepherd's pie and filled jacket potatoes. Sandwiches are available in the evening.

HAMPTON COURT
King's Arms

Lion Gate, Hampton Court Road

✖ lunchtime and evening; separate restaurant

🍴 seats on pavement

🍺 **Adnams Bitter; Hall & Woodhouse Badger Best Bitter, Tanglefoot; Wadworth 6X, Farmer's Glory**

🚂 Hampton Wick

Places to see: Hampton Court Palace and ground, Bushy Park

The King's Arms must have the finest position in London. It stands next to and within the shadow of the great Lion Gates entrance to Hampton Court, the palatial Tudor stately home built in rolling grounds in 1515 by Cardinal Wolsey and bequeathed to Henry VIII; opposite is the broad sweep of Bushy Park. The pub, once a hotel and formerly owned, according to a notice on the outside, by Hodgson's Kingston Brewery, has a fine black and white frontage with a porticoed entrance, two bowed sections either side of the main doors, and plants, ferns and a model stork above them.

The lounge is divided into sections. The main area, used chiefly by diners, has a large open fire in the bare brick wall, a shelf above it with stone jars and other bric-à-brac, low beams with dried plants hanging from them, and several high-backed wooden settles. The floor has a most impressive curved blue and white mosaic of tiny tiles. The bar is surmounted by a canopy of leaded lights and a frieze of hops.

The small room leading off has dark wood-panelled walls decorated with swords and a gun, an ancient flask in a wicker basket and a shelf displaying pictures of English monarchs. The small bar has a stunning canopy of leaded lights. Seats are made from old beer casks. Beyond this room is the large public bar, with bare boards, tables made from casks, an open fire with a mirrored mantel, hops hanging from the ceiling, a dartboard and bar billiards table.

The large servery in the main lounge offers a wide range of tasty dishes, including daily pasta and fish specials – fetuccine, gnocci, sea food salad – plus steaks, chicken Kiev, prawns in garlic butter, ploughman's and jacket potatoes. Meals are also served in an upstairs restaurant.

The broad pavement holds many trestle tables and bench seats surrounded by shrubs. Inside and outside, this ancient hostelry, lovingly maintained, fits snugly with the history and architecture around it.

TWICKENHAM
Pope's Grotto

Cross Deep

✖ lunchtime and evening

🍺 beer garden

◉ back dining section

🍺 **Young Bitter, Special Bitter, Winter Warmer**

A post-war roadhouse where anti-papists need not fear to tread; it is named after the poet Alexander Pope (1688-1744) who lived nearby. The pub sign shows him looking rather mournfully at a book; perhaps he was having problems with his scansion. When he was not composing poetry he designed and laid out a large grotto (now disappeared) and he later wrote a poem entitled "Verses on a Grotto by the River Thames at Twickenham, composed of Marbles, Spars and Minerals". He compared it to a "mine without a wish for gold" and suggested that only exceptional people should be allowed in; "Let such, such only, tread this sacred floor/Who dare to love their country, and be poor".

There are no such restrictions on customers to the pub, with trees and shrubs on the forecourt and a large bowed window in the centre of the two-storey building. Pleasant gardens opposite the pub slope down to the river. The Pope's Grotto has a rear terraced garden with tables and seats under trees, and a summer barbecue. Further seats are provided outside on the front terrace.

The main lounge is enormous, running to left and right of a vast rectangular bar. A small raised section beyond a balustrade is used by diners and families. The ceiling is pale green, matched by a patterned wallpaper. Chairs and sofas are upholstered in green and there are lamps everywhere – in window alcoves, on pillars and above the bar.

The spacious front section has curved and upholstered wall settles, a log-burning fire with a copper hood and above it a reproduction of Manet's painting "The Bar at the Folies Bergères", which shows two bottles of Bass; it is

🚃 Strawberry Hill

Places to see: Riverside, Twickenham rugby ground

165

decent of Youngs to advertise a rival brew. In sharp contrast, the tiny little snug bar in the bow window, with its own counter and curved wall seats, is intimate and has an almost rural feel.

Food, from a servery at the back of the main lounge, is wide-ranging and imaginative; the daily choice is chalked on blackboards held by effigies of a rather disdainful looking Alexander Pope. There is a roast beef carvery, plaice Kiev, plaice with broccoli and cheese filling, cheese and onion quiche, steak and kidney pie, burgers, and ploughman's.

Twickenham is the home of English Rugby Union football, with the world-famous ground known affectionately as "Twickers".

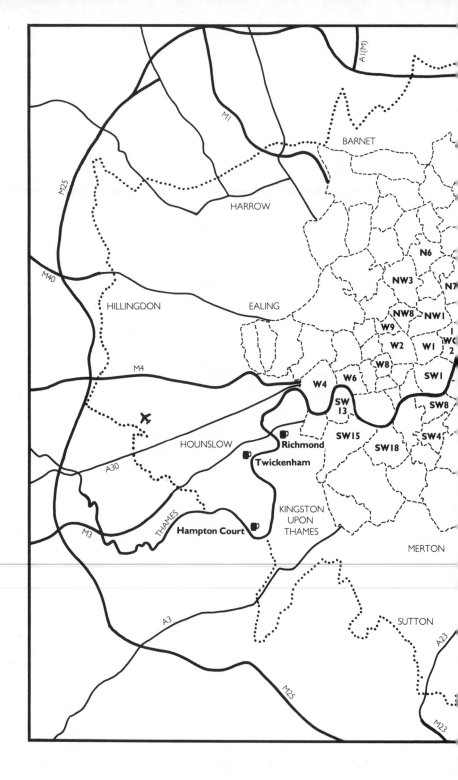

Numbered postal districts contain recommended pubs

ENFIELD

A10

M25

M11

A12

A127

REDBRIDGE

HAVERING

E5

E8 E9

NI

EC 2
4
3

SE1

SE16

E14

E6

BARKING

THAMES

A13

SE10

SE5

SE3

BEXLEY

A2

Croydon

BROMLEY

M25

M20

M26

miles   0   3
kilometres 0   5

Perrott Cartographics

ALMA BOOKS

Alma Books Ltd is the publishing company set up by CAMRA (the Campaign for Real Ale) to produce titles of interest to pub-lovers, beer-drinkers, tourists and travellers. A series of regional pub guides is being developed, along with other titles covering the United Kingdom as a whole.

For more information about Alma Books and to obtain the books listed below (which are also available at all good bookshops), write to Alma Books Ltd., 34 Alma Road, St Albans, Herts. AL1 3BW.

Available now:

The Best Pubs in Devon and Cornwall   £4.95
The Best Pubs in Lakeland   £3.95
Companion volumes to the London guide offering the reader detailed descriptions of the finest pubs in the area.

The Good Pub Food Guide   £5.95
Over four hundred pubs around the country where good food is as much a priority as good beer and you may find some of the best examples of traditional British cooking, using the finest local produce.

Pubs For Families   £4.95
A nationwide listing of pubs which serve real ale, where children are not just tolerated, but really made welcome by providing good facilities including meals and play areas (indoors as well as outside).

Forthcoming attractions:
The Bedside Book of Beer
A Complete Guide to the Great British Pub

Join CAMRA

If you like good beer and good pubs you could be helping in the fight to preserve, protect and promote them. CAMRA was set up in the early seventies to fight against the mass destruction of a part of Britain's heritage.

The giant brewers are still pushing through takeovers, mergers and closures of their smaller regional rivals. They are still reducing the availability and diluting the quality of a magnificent and uniquely British product – real ale. They are still trying to impose national brands of beer and lager on their customers whether they like it or not, and they are still closing down town and village local pubs or converting them into grotesque 'theme' pubs.

CAMRA wants to see genuine free competition in the brewing industry, fair prices, civilised licensing laws, and, above all, a top quality product brewed by local breweries in accordance with local tastes, and served in pubs that maintain the best features of a tradition that goes back centuries.

If you are in sympathy with these aims you could be expressing that sympathy in a positive way, by joining CAMRA. We have well over 20,000 members and that's not including our three fully paid-up dogs and two cats! Yet we're pitting ourselves against the power and financial muscle of a multi-million pound, multi-national industry. We desperately need active campaigning members, but we are also grateful for the support of people whose only involvement may be to pay their membership subscription once a year. It's only £9, but each additional subscription helps us to campaign that bit more effectively across the whole spectrum of pub issues on behalf of *all* pub-users.

If you leave it to others, you may wake up one day to find *your* local pub shut, *your* local brewery closed down, *your* favourite beer no longer being brewed. So join CAMRA and help us to prove that the most important person in the brewing industry isn't the megalomaniac chairman of some brewing giant, but that most vital, and under-valued person – the pub customer.

Full membership £9 Joint husband/wife membership £9 Life membership £90
I/We wish to become members of CAMRA Ltd. I/We agree to abide by the memorandum and articles of association of the company. I/We enclose a cheque/p.o. for £9/£90.

Name(s) _____

_____

Address _____

_____

_____

_____

Signature(s) _____

CORRECTIONS AND AMENDMENTS

Every year sees around a third of London pubs change hands. A new licensee can bring improvements or disaster to even the finest establishment. While most details were checked shortly before going to press, errors will inevitably occur and changes come thick and fast.

If you come upon listed pubs which have been ruined or if you find an undiscovered gem on your travels, let me know and I will investigate for the next edition.

Complete the forms or write to: Roger Protz (London), Alma Books, 34 Alma Road, St. Albans, Hertfordshire, AL1 3BW.

County _____

Town or village _____

Name of pub _____

Address _____

Location (A or B road) _____

Tel no. _____ Name of licensee _____

Description of pub (including bars, food, family room and any special facilities)

_____

_____

_____

_____

_____

Beers _____

_____

_____

_____

_____

Reasons for recommendation for inclusion in/deletion from the guide

_____

_____

_____

_____

Your name and address _____

_____

Postcode _____

County _____

Town or village _____

Name of pub _____

Address _____

Location (A or B road) _____

Tel no. _____ Name of licensee _____

Description of pub (including bars, food, family room and any special facilities)

_____

_____

_____

_____

_____

Beers _____

_____

_____

_____

_____

Reasons for recommendation for inclusion in/deletion from the guide

_____

_____

_____

_____

Your name and address _____

_____

_____

Postcode _____

County _____

Town or village _____

Name of pub _____

Address _____

Location (A or B road) _____

Tel no. _____ Name of licensee _____

Description of pub (including bars, food, family room and any special facilities)

_____

_____

_____

_____

Beers _____

_____

_____

_____

Reasons for recommendation for inclusion in/deletion from the guide

_____

_____

_____

_____

Your name and address _____

_____

_____

Postcode _____